NOT

yet

WHOLE

A Guide to Self-Understanding
and the End of Becoming

River Crane

Not Yet Whole:
A Guide to Self-Understanding
and the End of Becoming

© 2026 River Crane.

This book is intended for educational purposes only. It is not a substitute for professional medical, psychological, or therapeutic advice. The reader assumes full responsibility for their own understanding and application of the material presented. The author assumes no liability for any outcomes resulting from the use of this book.

Be your own light, and it will elevate everything it touches.

ISBN 979-8-9958588-0-5
ISBN 979-8-9958588-1-2
ISBN 979-8-9958588-2-9

River Crane
May 2026
Salt Lake City, Utah

Cover design: Kam Bains @kamthedesigner
Edited by: Lanette Sweeney

To David Bohm and J. Krishnamurti, whose dialogues inspired me to write this book.

For those who are ready to be their own light.

Reader Reflections

"River Crane's book *Not Yet Whole* is unusually clear in communicating a wholly understandable blueprint of how we operate as human beings. Recognizing that blueprint gives us the power to choose our experience. What is truly astounding about the work is the non-judgmental simplicity that comes forth in the straightforward examples and suggestions for contemplation, the doing of which causes a real shift away from attachment to the illusions we suffer under. I am looking forward to sharing it with those I love. Not only that, but I want to read it again myself, so I can convey her insights with others who I feel would also benefit from releasing the grip of suffering in their lives."

— *Tom Wright www.a-course-in-shamanism.com*

"River Crane has written a moving, thought-provoking book to help all of us recognize and see past the patterns of thought and behavior we've developed. Though our triggers and patterns have been reinforced like grooves in a record, Crane gently shows how we can live differently, aware enough to observe ourselves moment by moment and, perhaps, make new choices. Reading this brief book may prove life-changing; I highly recommend it."

— *Lanette Sweeney*

Author of *What I Should Have Said: A Poetry Memoir about Losing a Child to Addiction*

CONTENTS

A Note from the Author

____

After the birth of my second child, my life became unexpectedly challenging.

My body was in constant pain. A good night's sleep became more of a dream than a reality. A quiet exhaustion followed me through each day, and life began to feel dull and hollow. I searched for answers wherever I could—doctors, chiropractors, acupuncture—yet no one could tell me why I felt so terrible, nor when it would end.

At some point, something shifted within me. A quiet conviction arose. I cannot explain where it came from, only that it felt right. I sensed that I needed to take responsibility for my own healing—not just physically, but at the root.

So I turned my attention within.

I became determined to create a sacred space for myself. Each morning, I woke at 4 a.m. and committed two hours to being fully present with myself. The first hour, I sat in stillness, eyes closed, allowing my attention to move inward. This was followed by 30 minutes of physical movement, then 30 minutes of reading.

I did not skip a day. No matter how uncomfortable it felt in the beginning, I stayed with it. I committed to this rhythm for at least a year—without an end goal.

And one morning, something beautiful happened.

I opened my eyes, and I could feel something was undeniably different. A surge of energy moved through me—I felt alive, expansive, and deeply present, as though every cell in my body had awakened. Beyond the physical sensation was something far more profound: a deep sense of love and wholeness that I had never experienced before.

My experience of myself as whole and filled with and surrounded by love was not an idea, nor something I was trying to reach. This new awareness had simply emerged.

Over the years, I had read and heard about experiences like these—moments that would arise and then fade, often leaving people confused or searching for a way to hold onto that glimpse of wholeness. But what I was experiencing was not like that.

Something in me had shifted at a deeper level.

From that day forward, whenever my mind became still—even in the simplest moments, such as when looking at the sky or watching a pot of boiling water—I could feel an openness within me, a quiet, grounded presence. I lived with a sense of being whole and a deep gratitude for feeling so alive.

As I continued to observe, inquire, and reflect on my own and others' experiences—alongside what I had studied for more than a decade in psychology, brain development, trauma, human behavior, the mind-body connection, and therapeutic practices—something became increasingly clear:

Self-understanding is the foundation of clarity, wisdom, and wholeness.

My mind no longer functioned in the same way. Things that used to trigger me lost their grip. Old habits that used to trap my attention lost their power. People and things that used to disturb my mind no longer occupied my mental space. Internal conflict and indecisiveness were replaced with clarity and confidence.

For the first time, I felt whole and complete as I was. I did not feel I was perfect, nor was I striving for perfection. I did not feel I was beyond experiencing challenges. But I felt grounded, open, and fully alive.

Life, of course, continues to move. I still experience moments of stress, overwhelm, and emotional intensity—especially as a mother raising two children without extended support. But something fundamental has changed in how I meet those moments.

I have discovered a quiet confidence beneath all my actions— a steady knowing that I can face whatever arises with clarity and presence.

What I came to see is this: the more deeply I understand myself, the more naturally I am able to understand others. The more attuned I become to my own inner world, the easier it is to connect with people in a genuine, meaningful way. The more I accept myself as I am, the more able I am to love others as they are.

This book was born from that realization.

You cannot give what you do not yet have.

From the moment something within me opened—both in mind and in heart—I knew there was something here worth understanding and worth sharing.

I am not here to promise transformation.

I am here to offer clarity.

Because what I have come to see is simple, yet often overlooked:

Real transformation does not come from trying to become someone else. It comes from deeply understanding who you already are.

But to understand the self, we must first see clearly how the "self" is formed—how it operates, how it reacts, and how it shapes our experience of life.

That is the intention behind this book: To help you see clearly. To help you understand the structure of your own mind so that you can move through life with less reactivity, more clarity, and a deeper sense of wholeness.

If this is something you value, then this book was written for you.

May you feel whole, alive, and at ease within yourself.

~

You may be wondering what became of the pain that once caused me so much suffering. There was a time when my body went through intense physical challenges—severe back spasms that left me immobilized, sciatic pain that felt like a constant pull through my leg, and a frozen shoulder that limited my movement and deprived me of sleep. But the physical pain was not the hardest part. The exhaustion that followed me through each day, and the guilt and shame of not being able to show up fully for my family, hurt more than anything my body was going through.

These experiences were real and, at times, overwhelming.

Something began to shift when I turned inward with a sense of full responsibility—not just for fixing the symptoms, but for understanding myself more deeply.

Over time, all the pain gradually faded. What once felt constant is no longer present, and when discomfort does arise, it tends to resolve on its own.

I cannot say with certainty what caused these changes. But I sense that something fundamental moved when I began to approach my mind and body with clarity, attention, and responsibility.

~

If there is one thing I ask of you, it is this: Approach this book with sincerity.

Read it not for information, but as an invitation to look within—not casually, but with genuine attention—because what you may discover is not something new, but something you have never fully understood—now ready to be seen clearly.

Disclaimer

The observations in this book emerge from my direct inquiry into lived experience, supported by more than a decade of study in psychology, brain development, and consciousness.

These insights are informed not only by study and reflection, but also by my training as a licensed Rapid Transformational Therapist (RTT) and by years of observing the structure of the self unfolding in everyday life.

My conclusions are not presented as clinical findings. This book does not argue from academic authority nor cite studies as proof. My claims cannot be argued with nor disproved from the outside, because they point entirely inward. What this book describes can be verified only one way: **through your own direct experience.**

That is not a limitation of this book; it is its entire point.

If something written here corresponds to what you can observe in yourself—in your movement of thought, the activation of your conditioning, or the automatic quality of your reaction—then it is true for you in the only way that matters. If it does not resonate this way, set the book aside.

No belief is required. No authority is being claimed.

Only attention.

The path to wisdom is through self-understanding.

Be your own light and let that light elevate everything it touches.

Introduction

The Watchmaker's Mind

When was the last time you truly understood how something worked—not how to use it, not what it produced, but how it actually functioned from the inside out?

Imagine someone curious about watches who buys a beautiful timepiece and wants to understand it.

Most people would read the instruction manual. They'd learn which button sets the time, how to wind it, and how to adjust the date. They'd operate the watch successfully. Their understanding would be functional and limited, and they would decide that was enough.

A rare few might go deeper. They wouldn't just read the manual—they would take the watch apart. Carefully, piece by piece, they'd dismantle the entire mechanism. They'd examine each component: the mainspring that stores energy, the escapement that releases it in precise intervals, the gear train that transfers motion, and the balance wheel that regulates timing. They'd see how every part connects, how the whole system operates, how this intricate mechanism results in telling time.

Those who can reassemble the watch and restore it to its original function once they understand it completely will have gained something profound. They won't just know the watch works. They'll understand why it works, what happens when it doesn't, and what no amount of reading the manual could have shown them.

They will be the true watchmakers—not because they memorized more, but because they understood the complete mechanism.

This book is about a different kind of mechanism—the one that operates beneath every thought, every reaction, every sense of self. The lack of understanding of this inner mechanism creates the experience of feeling incomplete.

Your mind is a mechanism that sustains the sense that wholeness is somewhere ahead—always glimpsed, never quite arrived at, perpetually deferred to a better version of yourself that hasn't appeared yet.

Complete understanding of how your inner mechanism works is what allows wholeness to be lived, rather than visited.

WHO THIS BOOK IS FOR

If you are reading this, you have likely already tried many things—practices, methods, systems promising clarity or change.

You are not a beginner. You have read the books, followed the practices, and attended the courses or retreats. You have worked with therapists, explored mindfulness, perhaps tasted moments of genuine clarity or spaciousness that felt more real than anything you had previously known.

And yet something essential remained incomplete.

Perhaps you experienced a moment of profound clarity—a glimpse of something beyond the ordinary, restless sense of self—but afterward found yourself unable to live consistently from the space where you felt utterly alive and whole. Perhaps you have practiced for years and can access stillness in meditation or on retreats, but you find your clarity collapses the moment you step back into ordinary life, into the same relationships, the same pressures, the same patterns.

Perhaps you are simply exhausted by the gap between what you understand intellectually and what you can actually sustain in daily experience.

This is not because you haven't tried hard enough, nor because you need a different method or a better practice. You feel incomplete because you have never thoroughly understood the mechanism that creates your sense of incompleteness. And without complete understanding, every approach—however sincere, however well-designed—works at the surface while leaving the structure beneath it intact.

This book was written for the reader who has done the work, has seen glimpses of what is possible, and is ready to understand what is actually operating beneath it all.

If you have not yet glimpsed what is possible—if wholeness remains a concept rather than something you have already touched—this book is not your next step. It is written for those who know the territory but have not yet discovered how to live from that place of wholeness consistently.

WHAT THIS BOOK DOES—AND DOESN'T—DO

This is not another book about mindfulness, meditation, or spiritual development, nor is it another entry in the library of approaches you have already explored.

This book exposes the structure beneath what you know—the mechanism that has been operating continuously, whether or not you were aware of it, generating your experience of incompleteness moment by moment.

Most approaches work at the level of behavior, habits, and beliefs. Other authors assume the self is fundamentally sound but needs refinement: more consistent practice, clearer boundaries, sustained effort toward a better version of what you already are. Those self-help writers are attempting to rebrand the self as the solution.

This book asks a more fundamental question: what is the self in the first place, and how is it being created moment by moment?

Rather than adding techniques, this book removes confusion. Rather than teaching you what to do, it helps you see what is already happening—the structure, the conditioning, the automatic processes that generate thought, emotion, and identity beneath the conscious level.

Understanding the structure of the self does not give you control over it. Knowing how the self works dissolves the confusion that made your control seem necessary in the first place.

THE MECHANISM OF BECOMING

The subtitle of this book is *A Guide to Self-Understanding and the End of Becoming.* Those last four words deserve careful attention.

The self, when examined directly, shows itself to have one constant activity: becoming. Becoming is the continuous internal movement from what one is now to what one feels one *should be*—the constant push toward improvement, correction, refinement, and arrival. Becoming feels like the appropriate response to recognizing that something is not yet right. Becoming feels like the responsible path forward. But becoming is not the path to wholeness. Becoming is the part of the structure that prevents wholeness from emerging.

This requires extra explanation because it runs counter to everything the culture teaches us about growth and change.

The self exists in the internal movement between what I was, what I am, and what I feel I must become. The self lives in transit, always referencing the past as evidence, always projecting toward the future as a destination, never able to settle in the present moment. The self's striving movement is so constant, so familiar, that it is experienced not as a process but as reality.

But the present moment—where life is actually unfolding—is the one place the self cannot fully inhabit. The self is always a step behind or a step ahead, always interpreting what just happened or projecting what should happen next, never simply being here.

And wholeness is only ever *here*.

The project of becoming is never completed. Every step toward one's future version creates a new gap between this moment and what comes next. The self that is doing the becoming requires incompleteness to sustain itself—a self that arrived would have no function. So arrival is perpetually deferred. The becoming continues. The wholeness remains something glimpsed in moments but not lived consistently.

Becoming pauses not when something is finally achieved, but when the movement of becoming is seen clearly enough that its urgency ceases. Wholeness is not what you arrive at after becoming. Wholeness is what's possible when the mechanism of becoming is fully understood.

This book does not offer a better way of becoming. It offers something entirely different: a complete understanding of the mechanism that makes becoming feel necessary—and the direct recognition that eternally becoming will never get you to your destination.

THE DIFFERENCE BETWEEN INTELLECTUAL UNDERSTANDING AND SEEING

There is a distinction this book will return to again and again, because it determines whether what follows remains conceptual—or becomes something directly seen. This difference is worth introducing here.

Intellectual understanding is what accumulates in memory. You can understand the loop of conditioning with great precision—understand that thought is automatic, that the self is constructed through repetition, that identification with the self-image creates suffering—and still be completely captured by the loop the next time it activates. Intellectual understanding exists as knowledge. Knowledge is available when the system is calm. When identity feels threatened and emotion rises, knowledge steps aside and identification returns as if nothing had ever been understood.

Seeing is different. Seeing is a direct perception of the mechanism as it operates—at the moment thought rises, not afterward when it is safe to examine. Direct perception does not add information. Direct perception changes the relationship to what is seen. When the thought "I am not good enough" is recognized as a conditioned pattern repeating rather than a truth being reported, it loses its authority—not because it has been replaced with a better thought, but because the misidentification that gave it authority has been interrupted.

Insight is not a better version of understanding. Insight is a seeing that changes the brain's relationship to what has been recognized. Real change happens through insight in the present moment—instantaneously. Not through accumulating more knowledge. Not through effort applied toward future improvement. Insight is always now.

Reading this book conceptually will allow you to accumulate knowledge and sharpen your intellect. Reading it experientially—staying with each section until it points to something observable in your own direct experience—can lead to insight. And insight, not knowledge, is what opens up space for real change.

HOW THE BOOK IS STRUCTURED

I've divided this book into three parts. Each section builds on the previous—not by adding information, but by removing layers of confusion until what remains is direct perception rather than interpretation.

Part One dismantles the mechanism of the self completely. It examines how thought operates automatically from memory, how the brain stores and reinforces patterns, how the body executes signals faithfully, how the self emerges as repetitive thought, and how these components form a closed loop that sustains the sense of incompleteness without conscious direction. This first section also introduces the central insight about becoming: the self lives in the past and the future and has no access to the present. When thought stops, the self ceases—briefly, quietly—and something else is possible.

Part Two addresses the gap between understanding the mechanism intellectually and seeing it operate directly in lived experience. It examines what blocks direct perception, why effort prevents clarity rather than producing it, why the self cannot see itself, and what insight actually is and how it differs from accumulated understanding. This is where the distinction between knowing and seeing becomes the central territory—and where readers are invited to meet the mechanism not as a concept but as something directly observable in their own experience right now.

Part Three explores what ordinary life looks like when one sees the mechanism clearly enough that it no longer operates invisibly. This section does not describe enlightenment nor a permanent state; it describes wholeness recognized—not as something achieved after sufficient becoming, but as the natural condition of life when the confusion that obscures this recognition is finally cleared. This natural condition includes the unknown as direct experience, living from the space between the known and the unknown, the center of experience examined and found to be without independent substance, and relationship as the place where the dissolution of separation becomes most alive and most tangible.

HOW TO READ THIS BOOK

This book will not work as a manual nor a set of instructions. It cannot be skimmed for conclusions nor mined for techniques to apply later. This book asks for the same quality of attention you would bring to investigate anything precise and intricate. I am not asking for effort, only genuine interest in what is actually here.

Each section points you toward something in your own direct experience. The concepts are not the destination—they are fingers pointing at something that can only be verified by looking where they point. If you find yourself agreeing with an idea and moving on, pause. Agreement is still the intellect operating. The best question is always: can I observe this in myself, right now, as it operates?

There will be moments in reading when something lands—not as an idea understood but as a recognition of something already known but not yet named. Those moments are more important than anything else in the book. They are insight rather than understanding. Sit with them. Don't immediately convert them into a new framework or a new plan.

There may also be moments of resistance—places where the mind pushes back, where what is written conflicts with a deeply held belief about how change works or what the self is. Notice that resistance. Your pushback is the mechanism being described, operating in real time as you read. That noticing is not a distraction from the book. It is the book working.

> *Before continuing to Part One, take a moment and ask honestly: Do you have a sense, however quiet, that this book might provide something you are still missing— a method, an insight, or an understanding that will finally close a gap? Notice that feeling, not to dismiss it, but to see it clearly. Your striving is the movement of becoming; that movement is present right now, looking for the next thing to become. The book you are holding cannot give you wholeness. It can only help you see what has been obscuring it.*

THE WATCH IS IN YOUR HANDS

The watchmaker does not study the mechanism from a safe distance. To truly understand it, the watch must be taken apart. Component by component, the mechanism becomes visible— not as an abstraction, but as something directly seen.

That is what this book asks of you. Not to form a new belief. Not to agree or disagree. Not to adopt a new framework in place of the old ones. This book asks you to look at what is actually operating—in thought, in conditioning, in the self's continuous movement, in the relationship between becoming and the wholeness that becoming keeps just out of reach.

What you find when you look may be different from what you expected to find. It may be simpler. It may be more immediate. It may be closer than any path you have walked toward it.

The mechanism is about to become visible.

And what becomes visible—clearly, directly, without the distortion of what you think you should see—can no longer operate with the same invisibility.

PART ONE

The Mechanism Revealed

Understanding The Structure of The Self

CHAPTER 1

The Machinery of Thought

You are driving home.

*You're traveling the same route you've taken a
thousand times—past the gas station, left turn at
the intersection, the curve before your street.*

*And then suddenly, you're in your driveway
with no memory of the previous fifteen minutes.*

*Did you stop at the lights?
You must have.*

*Did you signal at the turns?
Of course. You're here after all.*

*The car is off.
The keys are in your hand.*

*But you recognize you weren't there
as you drove that last stretch.*

THE MOVEMENT OF THOUGHTS

You wake up suddenly at 3 a.m., and your mind is already running.

Did I send that email? What if they think I'm incompetent? I should have said it differently. Now they probably think I don't know what I'm doing. What if I lose this client? What if I lose my job? How will I pay the mortgage?

One thought triggers another. Then another. Before long, two hours have passed with you mentally rehearsing conversations that haven't happened and solving problems that don't exist yet.

You didn't choose to think these thoughts. They appeared. And once they started, they kept going—automatically, relentlessly, without permission.

Two completely different situations: one a physical routine, one a psychological spiral. But the same mechanism is running in both: your thoughts are operating entirely on their own, using material your brain has already stored, without asking you first.

This chapter is about that mechanism—not as a spiritual concept or a philosophical abstraction, but as a physical process happening in your brain right now, as you read these words.

Understanding your brain's automatic functioning is a necessary first step toward seeing everything this book reveals.

WHAT THOUGHT IS MADE OF

Thought is not a mysterious or spiritual phenomenon; it is a material process of the brain.

Neurons fire. Chemicals release. Electrical signals move through established pathways. Thought is as physical as a heartbeat or a breath—matter in motion, leaving behind what we recognize as thought.

But thought is distinct from other physical processes because thought is always made of the past.

Every thought you have ever had—every interpretation, every belief, every story about who you are—arose from memory. Experiences are stored in the brain using everything you already know and what has already happened to you. Thought has no other raw material. It cannot work with anything it has not already encountered. It can rearrange, recombine, project, and predict—but it cannot step outside what it already knows.

This is not a limitation unique to some people. It is the structural nature of thought itself.

Thought is always of the known. Always of the past. Always, in a precise sense, old.

"Right now, as you read this sentence, notice: a thought is arising. Did you choose it, or did it appear? Sit with that question for a moment. Not to answer it. Just to look.

THE CYCLE OF THOUGHT

To understand why thought operates the way it does, we first need to see how it forms.

This is not complicated once it is laid out plainly, but most people have never had the mechanism of thought explained to them—and without seeing this cycle clearly, the rest of what this book describes will remain abstract.

Each thought begins with an event. Something happens—in the world, in your body, in a conversation. The brain registers the experience. That experience is processed and converted into knowledge: a sense of what happened and what it means. Then, as the moment passes, that knowledge is stored as memory in the brain's neural networks.

Memory is not a passive archive. It is an active system. And the moment a new experience arrives that resembles something already stored, the brain retrieves the old memory instantly—often before conscious awareness has registered what is happening. That retrieved memory becomes the lens through which the new experience is interpreted. And so thought is generated not from what is actually happening now, but from what happened before.

The full cycle looks like this: **Event → Experience → Knowledge → Memory → Thought → Interpretation of the next event.**

Consider a simple example. You are driving and witness a car rush through a red light, then collide with another vehicle in the intersection. You experience yourself witnessing this event. You gain knowledge: that intersection is dangerous, and rushing through yellow lights can kill you. That knowledge is stored as memory. From that point on, every time you approach that same intersection, the memory activates automatically. You slow down. You become cautious. You may even feel a trace of anxiety—a tightening in the chest—before you consciously recall why.

In the future, you will not be responding to the intersection as it is; you will be responding to the intersection as it was the day you witnessed the crash there. The past will be governing your response to the present through the mechanism of thought.

This is not a malfunction. This is exactly how the system of thought is designed. The brain stores experiences to make future navigation more efficient. The problem is not the mechanism. The problem is that most of us do not know it is operating. We experience our interpretations as reality itself— not as a filtered version of reality that has been shaped by everything that has already happened to us.

THE SPEED OF REACTION

Neuroscience has revealed something worth pausing over: the unconscious mind reacts about half a second before conscious awareness even registers what is happening. By the time awareness arrives, the pattern has already fired. Your response was decided for you before you consciously chose it.

This is how reactions get mistaken for decisions.

You are walking down the street. Someone across the road looks like your ex-partner—the one from a relationship that left you hurt and wary. Before you are aware of anything, the mechanism is already in motion. Visual features match a stored memory. An old pattern activates. Emotional history floods in. Your body prepares: your heart rate rises, your stomach tightens, a trace of dread moves through your chest.

Only afterward does conscious awareness arrive: *Hold on—is that really David?*

And then you realize: it isn't. You spotted a complete stranger who happened to have features similar to David's.

But your body doesn't know that. It responded automatically, half a second before your awareness could verify anything.

By the time you notice anxiety, your body's reactions have already fired. By the time you notice offense, defense is already active. By the time you decide to hold back, withdrawal is already underway. What feels like a conscious choice is often awareness arriving late to a reaction already in motion—and then claiming the decision as its own.

This is the nature of a conditioned response. You are neither lazy nor weak. Your brain is doing precisely what it was built to do: move fast, protect continuity, and default to what is already known.

THOUGHT CAN ONLY WORK WITH WHAT IT ALREADY KNOWS

Thought can only work with what it already knows.

Because thought is made entirely of memory—of experience, past knowledge, past interpretation—it is structurally incapable of meeting the present as it actually is. It can only meet the present as you filter it through all your past experiences.

Something is happening right now, in this moment. But by the time thought arrives to interpret it, the moment has already passed through a filter built from everything that has happened before. What you experience as 'now' is, in large part, the past in new clothes.

This is not an occasional problem. It is the constant condition of a mind operating entirely through conditioned thought. The present moment—where life is actually unfolding—is the one place thought cannot fully reach. Your thoughts are always a fraction of a second behind, always interpreting by drawing on what has already been stored, always generating certainty from old data.

This is why thought prefers painful certainty to honest uncertainty. "I know I will fail" feels safer than "I don't know what's possible." "I know this person can't be trusted" feels safer than "What if he betrays me?" Certainty—even negative certainty—creates a feeling of control. The mind would rather be wrong and certain than open and genuinely unsure.

Thought's job is to reach backward into memory and pull out a conclusion that fits—not because your conclusion is accurate, but because belief in your accuracy is more comforting than uncertainty. The mechanism is efficient. It is also profoundly limiting.

THE OLD MANUAL

Consider a different kind of structure for a moment—one outside the mind entirely.

A senior manager makes every decision from an operating manual created twenty-seven years ago. He believes this manual is all he will ever need to run his department. He has memorized every detail of it. The manual once worked brilliantly. The world, however, has changed dramatically since then.

The manager knows this—at least intellectually. But change feels dangerous. The manual is familiar. It's what he knows. And the fear of operating without it feels more threatening than the increasingly poor results it produces.

So he keeps following it. Not because it still works, but because abandoning it would mean tolerating uncertainty. And uncertainty, to a mind organized around certainty, feels like the worst possible outcome.

This is precisely how conditioned thought operates.

Beliefs formed early in life—about who you are, what you deserve, whether you are safe, whether you are enough— become your manuals. They drive your behavior automatically. They shape your interpretations without being questioned. They do not ask whether the current situation actually resembles the original situation that gave rise to your thoughts about it. They simply execute.

A child who was harshly criticized early in life for making mistakes develops the belief that mistakes are dangerous. By adulthood, that belief is not experienced as a belief; it is experienced as truth. Every error, however minor, triggers the same internal response that was learned at age seven—not because the present situation is dangerous, but because the old manual says it is.

Nobody questions whether the response fits the moment. The system simply runs its old instructions, which have been reinforced by constant repetition.

The uncertainty that comes from updating the manual feels, to the conditioned mind, more dangerous than the misery the old manual produces. And so old patterns continue—meeting present situations with past solutions, again and again, with no awareness this is happening.

WHAT THOUGHT DOES
TO THE PRESENT MOMENT

Thought produces suffering—and the suffering is real. But there is a consequence more significant than the suffering itself.

When thought is active—pulling from memory, generating interpretation, seeking certainty— it occupies the space where direct perception could otherwise operate. Thought narrows attention inward toward: *what this means, how it relates to me, what happened before, what might happen next.* In that narrowing, what is actually happening right now becomes harder to observe.

You are in a conversation with someone you care about. They say something that activates an old wound. In an instant, thought has already generated an interpretation—*they don't respect me, this is exactly what always happens, I knew I couldn't trust him—*

and you are no longer in the conversation. You are in a reenactment of an older one, responding to a person who may not be doing what you think they are doing.

The person in front of you has become secondary to the story your thought is telling you about them.

This is the mechanism that blocks direct perception of what is actually happening. This reinterpretation of reality is not dramatic, and it is not obvious when it occurs. It feels, from inside it, exactly like reality. The interpretation feels like fact. The reaction feels like an appropriate response to what is genuinely happening.

But what is happening and what thought says is happening are not the same thing. And until that distinction is clearly seen, life is experienced primarily through a filter of the accumulated past—not through direct contact with what is actually here.

> *In this moment, is there any thought present about what you have just read? Notice it. Not to evaluate it— just to see that the thought has arrived and is already interpreting. The interpretation is made of memory. The reading itself was something else—direct contact with words on a page, before thought arrived to tell you what to make of them.*

THE MECHANISM REVEALED

Thought is an automatic, memory-driven process whose function is to interpret the present through the past—replacing the uncertainty of genuine unknowing with the comfort of familiar conclusions.

Thought arises without being chosen. It operates from stored experience. It generates interpretation before awareness arrives. It creates a sense of certainty, even false certainty, even painful certainty, because certainty feels safer than the unknown. And it cannot correct itself from within itself, because any attempt to use thought to examine thought is still thought using past experiences to examine thought.

Most psychological suffering does not arise from what is actually happening. Emotional pain arises from the thought's interpretation of what is happening—an interpretation generated in milliseconds from data that may be decades old, experienced as the simple truth of the present moment.

When thought says *I know I'm not good enough*, that certainty is believed, and helplessness follows. When thought says *I know this will end badly*, that certainty is believed, and resignation follows. When thought says *I know I can't change*, that certainty is believed, and the pattern continues, reinforcing itself, deepening the groove it has already worn.

These are not truths; they are protective mechanisms running on old instructions in a present moment thought cannot fully see.

When one's reliance on past experiences to interpret present moments is understood—not agreed with intellectually but actually seen in direct experience—something begins to change. Not through effort. Not by trying to think differently. But through the simple clarity of seeing the mechanism operating.

Seeing how thought distorts your reality is what this book is building toward. And your understanding begins here, with the recognition of what thought is, how it moves, and what it does to your experience of being alive.

WHO WAS DRIVING?

You arrived safely. Every light, every turn, every signal—executed perfectly by a system that never needed your conscious presence to function

That drive, completed without conscious awareness, involved your thoughts operating automatically from memory: faithful, efficient, and completely unconscious. Your unconscious is running the show all the time, not just while you're driving. Your unconscious operated in every conversation you have had today. Every reaction that arose before you decided to react, every conclusion you reached before you examined whether it was accurate, came from your unconscious.

Autopilot has been driving using a manual assembled from everything you have ever experienced—a manual you did not consciously write, one which you have, until now, largely not questioned (nor even realized was guiding you).

The question is not whether this mechanism exists. It does exist, in every human being, without exception.

The question is: **do you see that mechanism?**

Because the moment this mechanism is clearly seen—not as a concept to agree with but as a living process observed in your own experience—it stops operating invisibly. And that sudden seeing is where the lessons of this book begin.

CHAPTER 2

The Brain as Infrastructure

You walk into your childhood home after twenty years.

Your hand reaches left—and finds the light switch perfectly.

Your feet know which floorboard creaks, which stair is loose.

Your body turns toward the kitchen without conscious direction.

The house hasn't changed.

Neither has your brain's memory of it.

THE HOUSE THAT NEVER FORGOT

Nothing about this is deliberate. You did not retrieve a mental map, analyze your surroundings, nor calculate your movements. Your knowledge of the house lives somewhere deeper than conscious recall. Your spatial layout of the house is stored, preserved, and acted upon automatically—not by thought, but by the physical structure on which thought runs.

This is not thought at work. This is the brain.

The same phenomenon appears in smaller moments. You hear the first chords of a familiar song, and emotion rises in you before you've consciously registered what's playing. You hear a particular tone of voice, and your body tenses before your mind has processed a single word. You smell something and find yourself in a memory so complete it feels less like remembering and more like returning. These are not decisions. They are retrievals—stored patterns executing automatically, without permission or conscious direction.

In Chapter 1, we established that thought is a material process made entirely of the past—a movement of memory that generates interpretation, seeking certainty. But if thought operates this way, where are its instructions stored? Where do these patterns live when they are not actively running?

The answer is not philosophical. It is physical. Your instructions live in your brain.

MEMORY IS NOT WHAT YOU THINK IT IS

You're walking down the street when the smell of freshly baked bread reaches you. Without warning or effort, you're back in your grandmother's kitchen at age seven. You can see the countertop, feel the warmth of the oven, and hear her voice. The memory doesn't arrive as a story. It arrives as a total experience—sensory, emotional, immediate—before you have consciously decided to remember anything.

A smell—mere molecules entering your nose—has triggered a complete reconstruction of the past. That memory was stored somewhere physically and was retrieved in an instant. And that memory shaped your present experience before your awareness noticed what was happening.

Memory is not a narrative archive you consciously browse. It is a living, physical system that activates automatically whenever the present resembles the past.

This means that the past does not merely influence the present. It operates within it—silently, continuously, without asking permission.

When you understand this, you begin to see why so much of daily experience feels simultaneously familiar and slightly off—as if you are navigating the present through a map drawn from somewhere else. Because you are. The map is real. It is just old.

THREE POUNDS OF STORED EXPERIENCE

The brain is not mysterious. It is matter—roughly three pounds of physical tissue composed of about 86 billion neurons connected by trillions of synapses. Like your heart or liver, it is an organ with a unique, specific function—in this case, **to store experiences and convert them into responses.**

Every experience you have ever had—every sight, sound, touch, emotion, and thought—left a physical trace in your brain as a neural pattern. When neurons fire together repeatedly, they form pathways. These pathways are not symbolic or abstract. They are real and structural. They are matter, shaped by experience.

This is how your experience becomes memory, and memory becomes the lens through which every new experience is seen.

When you were in kindergarten, and your teacher criticized you in front of the class, that moment did not vanish when the school day ended. *The tone of her voice, the tightening in your chest, the thought "something is wrong with me," the embarrassment you felt*—all of it was encoded as neural connections. Those connections remain available decades later, ready to activate whenever the present resembles that moment. A certain tone of voice. A look of disapproval. The feeling of being judged.

The brain is not failing when this happens. Rather, it's just doing its job. Experience becomes knowledge. Knowledge becomes memory. Memory generates a reaction. The process is automatic, efficient, and entirely indifferent to whether the reaction still makes sense in the present situation.

THE BRAIN AS CORPORATE INFRASTRUCTURE

The earlier corporate metaphor now reveals its second component.

Thought functions as management with a fixed mindset—the automatic decision-making system running on outdated protocols. The brain functions as the corporate infrastructure—the building itself, where records are stored, routes are established, and operations run.

Imagine a large office building filled with filing cabinets, databases, electrical wiring, and hallways worn smooth from years of use. When management needs information, they don't invent it from scratch. They retrieve old records. When employees move through the building, they don't choose a fresh path each time. They follow established routes. The more a route is used, the easier it becomes to walk. Eventually, people move through the halls without thinking—the paths have become the defaults.

This is exactly how neural pathways form. A single experience creates a faint trail. Repetition deepens that path. Emotional intensity strengthens it. Over time, the trail becomes an unpaved road, then a highway. Eventually, the pathway fires automatically not because you chose it, but because it is the most worn route available.

This applies not only to practical skills like driving or typing, but to emotional and psychological patterns. A child who repeatedly experiences criticism learns, at the level of the nervous system, that mistakes are dangerous. By adulthood, the body reacts to minor errors as if something fundamental is at risk—not because the situation warrants it, but because the pathway of anxious fear was laid down long ago and has been reinforced ever since.

The problem is not that these pathways exist. The problem is when the pathways are invisible or are mistaken for reality.

When a learned pattern is confused with a permanent truth, the pathway becomes invisible. A historical event is experienced as a present danger. The interpretation is experienced as fact. And the self becomes defined by responses that no longer reflect what is actually happening.

The infrastructure itself is not to blame for this. It is simply doing what infrastructure does—running the routes that have been most traveled.

THE BUILDING IS NEUTRAL

The brain does not choose what it stores. The brain records what is repeated and what carries emotional weight. It does not decide which pathways to reinforce; it simply strengthens what is used. The brain does not question whether a response is still relevant. It runs what has been programmed.

The infrastructure is neutral. Faithful. Efficient.

The problem arises when a system designed to preserve the past is used to interpret the present without awareness. Old blueprints are treated as the current reality. The records from 20 years ago are retrieved to explain what is happening now.

This is not a flaw in the brain. Repetition and certainty are the brain's functions, operating without oversight.

Much of what feels permanent is simply learned. Much of what feels like truth is simply repetition. A response formed under duress at age nine feels, by adulthood, like the only possible response—not because it is, but because no other route has worn a pathway into the psyche.

Once this function is seen clearly, something begins to shift. Not because the infrastructure changes overnight, but because awareness introduces something the automatic system cannot generate on its own: the possibility of questioning whether the route being taken is the only one available.

Think of one belief you hold about yourself—
something that feels simply true, not like an
interpretation. Now ask: When did the pathway of this
belief first form? What experience created the original
trail? The belief feels like reality. But someone or
something laid the road from which you are drawing
that belief. And a manufactured road, in time, can be
seen for what it is.

THE INFRASTRUCTURE REMEMBERS

The childhood home is still there.

Your body moved through it without effort, without thought, without needing to remember consciously. The infrastructure of your brain stored everything faithfully, retrieved your muscle memories without judgment, executed your body's movements without questioning.

The problem is not the brain, which is doing its job perfectly. The problem is you are using programs written at another time, under different conditions, for a person who no longer exists in the same form, and those programs are running as if nothing has changed since the original memory formed.

Seeing how the brain works to make unconscious decisions based on your past experiences changes your relationship to your thoughts. The brain itself doesn't change. But when your relationship to your thoughts begins to change, however slightly, everything begins to loosen.

CHAPTER 3

The Body, the Executor

The alarm sounds—loud and piercing.

*Before you can form a thought, your body is
already moving.*

Your heart is racing.
Your breath is shallow.
Your legs are carrying you toward the door.

Then someone laughs.
"False alarm. Just a drill."

Your body didn't check.
It didn't pause to verify.
It didn't evaluate whether the danger was real.

*It executed immediately—faithful, responsive,
and innocent.*

THOUGHT INTERPRETS. BRAIN SIGNALS. BODY EXECUTES.

Imagine you are about to give a presentation at work. As you walk toward the conference room, your body starts to experience sudden changes. Your heart begins to race. Your palms grow damp. Your stomach tightens. Your throat feels dry. Your shoulders tense, and heat rises into your face.

You experience this collection of sensations and label it: *I am anxious.*

But there is no immediate physical threat. No danger in the room. No predator, no crisis, nothing that warrants a survival response. So why is the body preparing as if something fundamental is at risk?

The answer follows directly from what we've seen in the previous two chapters. Thought generates an interpretation—*I will be embarrassed if I fail*—and the brain recognizes that interpretation as danger based on stored memory from previous moments of exposure, judgment, or humiliation. Chemical and electrical signals are sent through the nervous system. The body receives those signals and executes them faithfully, producing the physical sensations you call *anxiety.*

The sequence is always the same: Thought interprets. Brain signals. Body executes.

Your body is not anxious. Your body is responding accurately to instructions it received—instructions shaped by thought and memory, not by what is actually present in the room. The process happens automatically, without conscious choice, in milliseconds, moment-to-moment.

THE BODY IS INNOCENT

The body is a biological organism—a living system composed of organs, muscles, tissues, cells, and chemical processes. It operates through finely tuned regulatory mechanisms that sustain life continuously, without requiring psychological involvement.

The body has no personal will. It has no opinions about what is happening. It has no psychological agenda. It does not interpret situations or construct stories about what events mean. It does not say, *this is happening to me.*

The body simply functions.

It responds to signals from the brain through built-in biological intelligence. The heart beats. The lungs breathe. The immune system responds. Wounds heal. Digestion adjusts. All of this occurs without identity, without narration, without a sense of self needing to be protected.

When the brain interprets a situation as dangerous, the body responds automatically—cortisol and adrenaline are released, heart rate increases, muscles tense, digestion slows, and blood flow is redirected toward the limbs. When the brain interprets a situation as safe, the body responds just as efficiently—heart rate slows, muscles relax, the system returns to baseline.

The body does not evaluate whether the signal it receives is accurate. It does not question whether the threat is real or historical. It does not consult present reality before responding.

It executes.

This reveals something that changes the entire relationship to physical sensation: function does not require identity. The body is not the source of psychological confusion. It is not broken. It is not malfunctioning.

The body is innocent. It is doing precisely what it was built to do, with perfect fidelity, every single time.

THE BODY AS WORKFORCE

The corporate metaphor now reveals its third component.

Thought is management with a fixed mindset—the automatic decision-making system operating on outdated protocols. The brain is infrastructure—the storage and processing center where records are filed and routes are established. And the body is the obedient workforce—the employees who receive directives and carry them out immediately, without evaluating whether the directive makes sense.

Management makes decisions based on old records retrieved from the filing cabinets. Instructions travel through communication channels. The workforce receives those instructions and executes them—immediately, faithfully, without question.

If management declares an emergency, the workforce mobilizes. If management announces all is well, the workforce stands down. The workforce does not evaluate whether the decision fits the present situation. It obeys orders.

Consider what this looks like in practice. A manager receives a message from a difficult client—the kind who has historically caused serious problems. Management immediately pulls the relevant files and sends out warnings: Danger. Protect the company. Respond defensively. The memo goes out. The workforce mobilizes: heart rate rises, shoulders tighten, voice sharpens, jaw clenches.

The client may simply be having a bad day and need a calm, direct response. But the workforce doesn't know that. The workers received their instructions from a management system consulting records from years ago—and they executed them faithfully.

This is the body's role in the mechanism. The body is not the source of confusion nor a problem to be solved. The body is simply the workforce, doing exactly what it was told, by a system that may not have checked whether the instructions are still relevant.

THE AUTOMATIC CHAIN

The complete sequence unfolds automatically, in milliseconds, beneath conscious awareness.

Thought generates an interpretation based on experience: *This is dangerous. I'm going to be humiliated. They're judging me.* The brain recognizes this interpretation as significant, consults stored memory, activates relevant neural pathways, and sends chemical and electrical signals through the nervous system. The body receives those signals and executes them immediately: heart rate increases, muscles tense, breath shortens, and sensations arise throughout the body.

You experience these physical sensations and label them as emotion: *I am anxious. I am angry. I am ashamed.*

The entire sequence completes before conscious awareness has registered what happened. By the time you notice that you feel anxious, the anxiety has already been running for half a second. By the time you decide how to respond, the body has already prepared for a threat that may exist only in memory.

Consider something as simple as sending an email to your manager. The moment you press send, thought fires: *What if they think this is a bad idea? What if they think of me as someone who lacks creativity?* Your brain retrieves memories of previous moments of criticism. Signals travel. Your stomach tightens. Your breath becomes shallow. Your body is already responding to a thought, about a possibility, regarding something that has not yet happened and may never happen.

Emotions are not mysterious internal states arising from nowhere. They are physical responses to thought's interpretations—the body faithfully executing instructions from a management system running on old records.

WHAT THE BODY HOLDS—
AND WHAT IT DOESN'T

There is a widespread and sincere belief that the body stores trauma—that painful experiences live inside physical tissue and must be actively released through bodywork, breath, or movement. This idea is well-intentioned, but it is not mechanically accurate.

Psychological memory is stored in the brain, encoded as neural patterns that replay during experiences, especially threatening or emotionally charged ones. When those patterns are activated by something in the present that resembles the original experience, the brain sends signals through the nervous system. The body then responds—now, in the present moment—to those signals.

From the inside, this can feel exactly as though the body is reliving the past. The sensations are real. The physical experience is genuine. But what is actually happening is memory activation in the brain, followed by signal transmission, followed by physical execution in the present.

Like a smoke alarm responding to a faulty sensor—the alarm is real, the sound is real, the response is real. But no fire is present. The sensor is misfiring based on old data.

If the body were literally storing trauma in its tissue, releasing it would require forcing the trauma out somehow. But the body is responding to present-moment signals—and signals can change. When the mechanism that generates them is understood, and when conditioned memory is no longer unconsciously activated in the same automatic way, the body settles on its own. Not because it was forced to release anything, but because the instructions it was receiving had changed.

The body simply responds. It was never the problem. It was always the messenger.

WHO SENT THE ALARM?

The alarm sounded. Your body moved instantly. The danger was false.

The body didn't verify.

It didn't question.

It executed faithfully—as it always does, as it is designed to do, with perfect efficiency and no psychological agenda of its own.

The body is not anxious by nature. It is not depressed by design. It is not made to be angry. It responds as it's been trained to every signal it receives.

The question, then, is never why the body reacts.

The question is always: who sent the alarm?

The next time a strong physical sensation arises—tightening in the chest, heat in the face, contraction in the stomach—pause for a moment before labeling it. Don't call it anxiety or anger or dread. Just notice the sensation itself as a pure physical experience. Then ask yourself: what thought preceded this? What interpretation generated the signal that the body is now executing? The body is not the origin. It is the display. And displays can be read.

CHAPTER 4

The Self

The company was young once.

Flexible. Willing to try anything.

Then the name went on the building.

Now every decision must protect the brand.

Every action must match "who we are."

Someone suggests a pivot.
"We don't do that. That's not us."

The name on the building became a cage.

WHO ARE YOU?

Thought is automatic. The brain stores. The body executes.

But something seems to sit at the center of all this—something that experiences anxiety, feels anger, carries inadequacy, regrets the past, and worries about the future. Something to which the thoughts appear to belong. Something that persists across all these moments as a kind of constant.

Who is the "I" that feels all of this?

Who is the "me" the thoughts seem to be about?

Who is this psychological entity that appears to be at the center of your entire experience—the one reading these words right now, the one who seems to have always been there?

This is not a philosophical question. It is the most practical question possible. Because the answer changes everything about how suffering is understood—and about whether it can end.

HOW THE "I" IS ASSEMBLED

When you say "I," to what or whom are you actually referring?

The answer comes quickly—and it comes as a description. Parent. Artist. Someone who tries hard but never quite makes it. Anxious. Successful. Not good enough. Reliable. Lost. These identities feel like facts. They feel like what you are, not like labels applied to you.

But notice what is actually happening. These are descriptions generated by thought. They are interpretations accumulated over time — stories about who this "I" is, based on what has happened, what has been said, what has been repeatedly thought. These descriptors are not what you are. They are what your thoughts say you are.

Watch how this assembly works in practice. Something goes wrong at work, and a thought arises immediately: I always make mistakes. That's just how I am. A relationship ends, and the interpretation arrives: I'm not the kind of person who can hold on to something good. I always attract the wrong people. Each experience adds another layer—another description, another label, another entry in the file marked "me."

Beneath all the labels, beneath all the descriptions, beneath all the identities—what actually is this "I?"

When looked at directly—not conceptually, but as lived experience—in this moment, no solid, permanent entity called "me" is found. What is found is a process. A movement in psychological time. A constant becoming. Something that exists only in motion, only in the act of referring to itself.

THE SELF LIVES IN PSYCHOLOGICAL TIME

The self is not a tangible thing.

It is not an entity sitting somewhere inside the body.

It is not a permanent "me" that was there at birth and will remain unchanged until death

The self is movement. Specifically, it is the movement of thought through psychological time, and that movement is what creates the experience of being a continuous "*me.*"

It is worth distinguishing between two kinds of time, because confusing them is the source of enormous unnecessary suffering.

Chronological time is real and necessary. Yesterday, today, tomorrow—the clock, the calendar, the appointment at three, the flight to catch, the year your child was born. This is functional time. It exists. It matters. Planning, learning from the past, honoring commitments—all of this requires chronological time.

Psychological time is different. It is the internal movement from *what I was to what I am to what I want to become.* It is the narrative the self tells itself about its own continuity—the story of becoming. And this is where the self actually lives: in the constant movement between past inadequacy and future improvement, between who you were and who you think you need to be, between what happened and what it means about you.

The self has no access to the present. It lives in transit—always referencing what was, always projecting toward what should be, always measuring the distance between them. The present moment, where life is actually happening, is the one place the self cannot fully inhabit. It is always a step behind or a step ahead, never simply here.

This is not an abstract observation. It is the lived experience of anyone who has ever lain awake at night replaying a conversation from the afternoon, or felt dread about something that hasn't happened yet, or found a quiet moment suddenly invaded by the feeling that more needs to be done to get somewhere they aren't yet, become something they aren't yet.

That movement—the restless, tireless becoming—is the self's natural state. It is not a problem to be fixed. It is the self's structure. It cannot do otherwise, because without movement, without becoming, the self has nothing to stand on.

HOW THE SELF FORMS:
THE MECHANICS OF IDENTITY

The formation of the self through repetition is almost mechanical. It follows the same cycle we saw in Chapter 1—**Event → Experience → Knowledge → Memory**—but now operating on the question of identity rather than simple pattern recognition.

At age seven, a teacher criticizes you in front of the class. A thought arises in that moment: *"I am such a loser."* That thought passes. But similar moments accumulate—another comparison, another failure, another confirmation of the same conclusion. Each one deepens the neural pathway. By adolescence, the thought runs in the background without needing an external trigger. By adulthood, it is no longer experienced as a thought. It has become an identity.

Not *"I think I'm a loser"*—which could be examined, questioned, held lightly.

Simply: *"I am a loser."*

By the time this identity is established, it is defended. Compliments are deflected or explained away. Evidence of capability is attributed to luck or extra effort. The identity of inadequacy is protected—not because it serves, but because it has become familiar. Because it has become "me" to the one who believes it. And to threaten "me" is to threaten something that feels like survival.

But *"I am a loser"* was never true. It was a thought that arose once at age seven, in a specific moment, in response to a specific person, under specific circumstances. Repetition gave it permanence. But repetition does not make something real.

If you repeat "I am a purple elephant" ten thousand times, you will not become a purple elephant, but you may believe you are. And belief, once embedded deeply enough, is experienced as fact.

The self is a belief—reinforced by repetition, mistaken for reality, and defended as if life itself depended on it.

Try to think of one identity you carry—something you believe you are. Not a role, but a quality: I am anxious. I am not creative. I am someone who struggles. Now ask honestly: when did this first appear as a thought rather than a fact? It was a thought once. Repetition made it your identity. Can you feel the difference between the thought and the thing it claims to describe?

THE BRAND THAT CANNOT QUESTION ITSELF

The corporate metaphor now becomes complete.

Thought is management with a fixed mindset—the automatic decision-making system operating on outdated protocols. The brain is infrastructure—storage, established routes, and the processing center. The body is the workforce—receiving signals and faithfully executing directives. And the self is company identity — the brand, the label, the internal story of who we are, the name on the building.

Company identity forms through repetition. A motto is chosen: *"We are an innovative company."* These words are repeated in meetings, in hiring interviews, in marketing. Over the years, the motto becomes the company's brand. The original statement is no longer a message; it is who the company is, its very identity. A decade later, that brand is defended—even when it is no longer accurate. The company hasn't genuinely innovated in years, but the identity must be protected, because the identity has become more real than reality.

The brand has no physical existence. You cannot touch it or find it anywhere in the building. It exists only as repeated messaging. Stop the messaging, and the brand fades. The building remains. The people remain. But the identity was always just an idea, reinforced through repetition, until it felt solid.

Blockbuster is a perfect example of what happens when identity becomes more important than reality. For years, the same structure was reinforced: We are the video rental company. Customers come to our physical stores. That's who we are. Then Netflix offered Blockbuster a partnership. Blockbuster refused—not because the market wasn't clearly shifting, but because streaming wasn't who they were. By 2010, Blockbuster filed for bankruptcy.

The illusion killed the reality.

The self carries the same structural risk. It is separative by nature—creating division between what I am and what I should be, between this version of myself and the better version I'm working toward. The self compares and judges because it can only know itself by measuring itself against something else. It is formed entirely from the past and can only respond to what it already knows. Everything is filtered through the question:

What does this mean about me? And it exists in perpetual conflict—always becoming, never arriving, always improving, striving toward a destination that keeps moving.

The self is the origin of psychological suffering. Not because something is wrong with you. Not because you are broken. But because suffering is structurally built into the self's design, necessary to keep you striving. This division creates conflict, becoming creates perpetual inadequacy, psychological time creates regret about the past and anxiety about the future.

Self-improvement does not end this suffering because improving the self actually strengthens the self. And the self, by its very structure, generates the struggle it is trying to resolve.

NO THOUGHT, NO SELF

Here is something worth looking at directly, rather than passing over quickly. The self exists only as thought in motion. It has no independent existence outside the movement of thought. It is not a thing that thought describes—it is what thought does when it refers to itself repeatedly enough to create the feeling of continuity.

This means something precise: **when thought stops, the self ceases to exist.**

Not forever. Not permanently. Just in that gap. In the space between one thought and the next—however brief—there is no self. There is only awareness, without anyone claiming it.

Most people have touched this without recognizing it. In the instant of waking, before the day's story assembles. In complete absorption in music or movement or nature—the moment before thought returns and says, *"I am enjoying this."* In genuine laughter, before it becomes a performance. In those moments, something is present that the self is not. Something aware, alive, and unburdened.

The self is not what you are. It is what thought makes you think you are. And it has been running your experience—quietly, continuously, beneath awareness—since long before you thought to question it.

AWARENESS IS NOT THE SELF

There is one more distinction this chapter must make, because everything that follows in this book depends on it.

In this moment, whatever is reading these words—whatever is aware of thoughts arising as you read, aware of reactions forming, aware of the internal commentary running—that awareness is not itself a thought. The self is constructed by the movement of thought. But what observes thought is not thought.

You can notice the thought *"I am not good enough"* without being that thought. Noticing and thought are not the same. Something is aware of the thought—and that something is not the thought itself.

Most of the time, this distinction collapses entirely. The awareness that could observe the thought becomes absorbed by it. You become the thought-created identity, the automatic pattern, the repetitive story. You lack the mental space to notice. That collapse—awareness losing itself in the content of thought—is what identification means. And identification, not thought itself, is the root of psychological suffering.

Thought will continue to arise. The brain will continue to retrieve. The body will continue to execute. But when the self is seen for what it is—a process, not a permanent entity; a movement, not a fact—something fundamental shifts in the relationship to all of it.

Not because the self is destroyed. Because it is no longer mistaken for what you are.

THE NAME ON THE BUILDING

The company was adaptive once, before the name went on the building, before the company's identity became rigid and defensive.

The self works the same way. It begins fluid. Then repetition solidifies certain patterns: *I am shy. I am the smart one. I am not good enough. I am the one who holds everything together.* The name goes on the building, and from that point on, every experience is filtered through the established identity. Every threat to the image is defended. Every possibility that doesn't align with who we are is rejected.

The self isn't fixed by nature. It is the repetitive thoughts that create the illusion of continuity—*I was this yesterday, I am this today, I will be this tomorrow.* Once believed completely, it becomes a prison whose bars aren't visible because they're made of thought.

Blockbuster died defending a brand identity that had become more real to it than the market it was operating in. The same movement appears in a life every time a genuine possibility is refused because it doesn't match who you think you are.

The self being protected isn't real. It is an idea, repeated so many times it feels solid. But it was never solid. The name on the building is just a label. The brand is just messaging. The self is just a thought moving, and movement, when seen clearly, does not have the same authority as solid ground.

The trap was never in the building. It was in the belief that the thought was the reality.

For one moment—not as an exercise, just as direct looking—notice what is aware of reading this. Not the thoughts about what you've read. The awareness itself. Can you find its boundary? Can you locate where it begins and where "you" ends? Or is there simply awareness open, present, without a center claiming it? This is not something to achieve. It is something already here, waiting to be noticed.

CHAPTER 5

———

The Closed Loop

The hamster runs,
and the wheel spins.

Each step creates the next step.

Each spin requires another.

Faster, faster.

The hamster believes
it's going somewhere.

But the wheel
has no destination.

THE COMPLETE MECHANISM

Four components have been examined separately. Now they appear together as a single self-sustaining movement.

Thought interprets, drawing from memory, generating meaning before awareness arrives. The brain activates the relevant pathways, retrieving whatever experience most closely resembles the present trigger. The body faithfully and immediately executes the signals it receives, without evaluating their accuracy. And the self—the psychological "me" formed through repetition—identifies with all of it, claiming the thought as its own, the sensation as proof of its condition, the story as the truth of what is happening.

This is not four separate processes occurring in sequence. This is one movement, happening simultaneously, completing itself before awareness can intervene.

And the movement is self-sustaining.

The self is formed through this repetition. It has no independent existence outside the loop—and yet it experiences itself as the one running the loop. This is the central confusion: the self believes it is the driver when it is actually the product. It believes it is responding to reality when it is mostly responding to its own previous responses, encoded as memory, retrieved as present truth.

You mistake the self for what you are. That misidentification is what makes a neutral comment feel like an attack, a minor failure feels like evidence of fundamental inadequacy, and ordinary uncertainty feel like an existential threat. Nothing is being distorted from the outside. The distortion is structural, internal, and invisible—until it is seen.

HOW THE LOOP RUNS

A thought arises—triggered by something in the environment or by internal movement. *"I am not good enough"* pulls the next thought behind it: *"I'm going to fail, and everyone will see."* This does not arise from choice. It arises from what is already stored—the accumulated pattern, firing along a pathway worn deep through repetition.

The brain recognizes the familiar sequence and consults its files: Failure means humiliation. Humiliation means danger. We have protocols for this. Pathways formed over the years activate quickly. Memory floods in, often entirely beneath awareness, so its impact is felt in the body before the mind has registered what is happening.

The brain signals the body. Chemical messengers are released, and the nervous system mobilizes: *prepare for threat.* The body executes faithfully. Heart pounds, palms sweat, stomach tightens, throat constricts. The body does not evaluate whether the threat is real or remembered. It obeys the signal.

Thought returns and labels the sensation: *I am anxious.* When that label is believed—when it becomes identity rather than observation—it becomes fuel. The sensation feels like confirmation. More thought follows, each adding another layer of certainty: *What if they laugh? What if I make a fool of myself? What if this proves what I've always suspected about myself?* Each repetition strengthens the identity and deepens the pathway.

Thought stirs sensation. Sensation intensifies thought. Thought strengthens the self. The self generates more thought. The loop repeats—faster, more efficiently, more invisibly than the time before.

A FULL CYCLE IN REAL LIFE

You wake at 7:00 a.m. Within seconds—before you are fully conscious—the system is already running. An old belief launches without announcement: *I am useless.* From it, thoughts appear: *Today is going to be hard. What's the point? I'm going to fail anyway.* No decision was made. No reasoning occurred. The program simply launched, as it has countless times on previous mornings.

The brain retrieves supporting evidence: past failures, past struggles, previous mornings that felt exactly the same. Pathways fire: This sequence is familiar. Prepare. Signals move into the body. Cortisol releases. The chest feels heavy. Muscles tense. A dull contraction settles in. The body is not choosing any of this. It is responding faithfully to instructions it has received hundreds of times before.

Thought interprets the sensations: *I'm depressed. I'm anxious. This day is going to be awful.* The sensation now feels like proof—not of a passing mood, but of something true about who you are and how your life is. And before the day has begun, the loop has already determined how the day will be experienced.

At 9:00 a.m., your boss sends a message: "Let's have a chat." Thought reacts in an instant: *Did I screw something up again? Am I in trouble?* No pause. No inquiry. Just automatic meaning-making from a system that cannot tolerate not knowing.

The brain identifies the familiar threat sequence and floods the system with memory: *an elementary-school teacher, your parent when you were 10, your last performance review.* The past rushes in to interpret a two-sentence message. The body responds as if the threat is confirmed: adrenaline surges, heart races, face flushes, hands sweat, stomach tightens.

The mechanism runs from interpretation, not from fact. Your boss wanted to reschedule a meeting. But the loop ran anyway—completely, convincingly, as if it were simply reality unfolding.

By the end of the day, this loop has not run once or twice. It may have run fifty, a hundred, two hundred times. Each cycle strengthens the next. It feels personal—deeply, undeniably personal—because it is not seen as a mechanism. It is experienced *as you.*

Nothing in this is a character flaw. Nothing here is moral weakness or insufficient effort. It is simply the system operating as designed when left unobserved

THE LOOP SUSTAINS ITSELF THROUGH BECOMING

There is a feature of the loop that makes it nearly impossible to exit from inside it—and seeing this clearly is essential.

The loop sustains itself through the movement of *becoming*.

Becoming is the self's natural activity. It is the constant internal movement away from what is and toward what should be. *I am not calm enough*, so I will practice becoming calmer. *I am not confident enough*, so I will work at becoming more confident. *I am not good enough*, so I strive at becoming better.

This movement feels like progress. It feels like the appropriate response to recognizing a problem. But look at its structure carefully: it begins by rejecting what is present, projects an improved version into the future, and creates a gap between here and there that the self must now spend its energy crossing.

That gap is where suffering lives. The movement of becoming does not close the gap—it maintains it. Every step toward the future version creates a new gap. The destination keeps moving. The self keeps becoming. The loop keeps spinning.

And here is the most important part: self-improvement is becoming, but reorganized into what looks like productivity. The structure is identical. *I am not enough as I am;* therefore, I must become something different; therefore, *I am working on it;* therefore, I am not yet there; therefore, *I am not enough*. The language of growth replaces the language of failure, but the underlying movement—rejection of what is, projection toward what should be—remains unchanged. This is why people can spend decades in therapy, sustained inquiry, contemplative practice, and still feel, in quiet moments, fundamentally the same. More informed. More articulate. Sometimes genuinely more self-aware. But still organized, at the deepest level, around *not enough yet*. Still becoming. Still running.

WHY SELF-IMPROVEMENT DOES'T WORK

Self-improvement is the self attempting to improve the self—part of the loop trying to end the loop using the loop's own mechanism.

Consider what actually happens when the effort begins. Thought identifies a problem: *I am not confident.* Immediately, the loop reorganizes around the new goal: *I need to become more confident.* The brain retrieves its familiar comparisons and evidence. The body receives the signal of inadequacy and tightens. Self-consciousness intensifies. Thought observes the discomfort and interprets: *I'm still not there.* I need to work harder. The surface looks like growth—books, routines, affirmations, practices. The structure underneath is the same loop, wearing new clothes.

The loop converts every experience into evidence for its own conclusions. Success after hard work confirms: *I have to work twice as hard just to keep up.* Failure confirms: *I knew I wasn't enough.* Even progress becomes fuel: *I'm improving, which means I wasn't good enough before, which means I'm still not quite there yet.*

The self-improvement project gives the loop something useful to do so that it feels like forward motion. And as long as the loop is productively busy improving itself, it never has to be fully seen for what it is.

THE LOOP CANNOT END ITSELF

The loop cannot end itself. This is not pessimism—it is precision. And understanding why it cannot end itself is what opens the door to what can actually happen.

It cannot end itself because it is automatic. The loop does not run by choice—it runs beneath awareness. By the time *"I am anxious"* is recognized as a label, the full sequence of thought, memory, bodily response, and identification has already been completed. Awareness arrives as a spectator after the fact.

It cannot end itself because the self trying to fix the self only strengthens the self. *"I need to stop being anxious"* is anxiety reorganized as a self-improvement project. The one doing the fixing is the same mechanism generating the problem. Each attempt creates another cycle.

The striving self cannot end itself because any action driven by identity reinforces identity. Meditation to eliminate anxiety. Affirmations to manufacture confidence. Therapy to fix what's wrong with me. All of these can, and often do, quietly preserve the same structure: a self that is inadequate now and must become something better in order to feel better. The methods change and occasionally help. The underlying loop continues under a more respectable name.

The hamster is not broken. The wheel is not broken. The hamster is simply inside the wheel, mistaking circular motion for forward progress—and the wheel is designed to feel exactly like a path going somewhere.

WHAT ACTUALLY CHANGES

The loop cannot end itself. But something else is possible— and it does not come from inside the wheel.

What changes is seeing. Not understanding the loop in the conceptual sense, many people have remained entirely inside it. Seeing means direct perception of the mechanism as it operates, at the moment it happens, without the self standing between the observer and the observed.

When the loop is understood as a loop—when "*I am not good enough*" is recognized as a conditioned thought repeating rather than a fact being reported; when memory is seen retrieving itself to interpret the present; when the body is recognized as executing faithfully rather than expressing fundamental truth; when the self is seen as a process rather than a permanent entity—the spell begins to weaken. Not because anything has been fixed. Because something has been seen.

The loop will still run. Thought will still arise. The body will still respond. The self will still appear. But what was invisible is now visible—and what is seen clearly cannot hold the same authority it held in the dark.

This is not a new technique. It is not another form of becoming. It is the end of a specific confusion that mistakes the loop for reality, the process for identity, the automatic response for a decision. And seeing the process as it occurs, quiet as it is, changes what is possible next.

INSIDE THE WHEEL

The hamster cannot see the wheel from inside the mechanism. Each step feels purposeful. Each spin feels like progress. The destination remains just ahead.

The wheel keeps spinning, not because you are failing. It spins because it is designed to spin—its function is to keep the self in motion, becoming better, finally arriving, while the arrival is structurally prevented by the movement itself.

Look at the mechanism plainly: thought arises from memory; the brain activates the pathway; the body executes the signal; the self identifies with the result; and thought is strengthened. Each component is innocent. Each component does exactly what it was built to do. Nothing wrong. Nothing personal. Just machinery operating as designed.

The hamster isn't broken. The wheel isn't broken.

You have simply been inside it—mistaking circular motion for forward progress, and the wheel for the world.

The Edge of the Known

The mechanism is now visible—not as theory, but as something that can be verified directly in experience.

Thought interprets automatically from memory, seeking certainty even when certainty creates suffering. The brain stores experience as neural pathways, retrieving the past to interpret the present. The body faithfully executes signals, creating the physical sensations labeled as emotion. The self—the psychological "me"—is repetitive thought moving through time, sustained by the constant activity of becoming, mistaking that movement for being.

When these four components work together, they form a closed loop. Thought stirs sensation. Sensation intensifies thought. Thought strengthens identity. Identity reinforces thought. The cycle runs beneath awareness, generating the continuous experience of "me" and "my suffering"—automatically, efficiently, without anyone choosing it.

This is conditioning. Not moral weakness. Not a character flaw. Not the result of insufficient effort or the wrong approach. Conditioning is accumulated programming—beliefs, patterns, interpretations—operating automatically, beneath the level of conscious decision-making.

> *The loop that produces the experience of being not yet whole is not a personal failing. It is a structure. And a structure, once clearly seen, no longer has the same invisible authority.*

When the structure is seen clearly, it stops being interpreted as you.

When "*I am anxious*" was believed to be a fact about who you are, anxiety felt personal, permanent, and overwhelming. Now it can be seen as a process: **thought interpreting, brain signaling, body responding, self identifying**. The experience may still arise—the loop may still run. But the relationship to it has shifted. There is space where there was none. Observation where there was only identification.

The self cannot see the self from within its own structure. Effort from inside the loop strengthens the loop. This is why self-improvement fails at the deepest level—not because the effort is insufficient or the approach is wrong, but because improvement is the self attempting to become something other than what it is, using the same mechanism that generated the problem. The movement of becoming is itself the structure that prevents arrival.

Before continuing, let's pause here.

Not to review what has been understood. Not to consolidate or organize. But simply to notice what is happening right now, in this moment, as you read.

A thought has likely arisen about what you've just read—perhaps you're experiencing recognition, perhaps resistance, perhaps the quiet sense that something familiar has been named. Notice that thought. It arose from memory. It is the mechanism described on these pages, operating right now as you attempt to understand it.

The loop you have just read about is the one you just used to.

That is not a problem. It is the starting point. Because once the mechanism is noticed in real time—not as a concept being agreed with but as something directly observed—something is already different.

> *"Knowing happens in thought. Seeing happens in awareness. Knowing changes what you think about yourself. Seeing changes how you relate to yourself."*

The known is everything thought has accumulated—every belief, identity, memory, and interpretation. It is the entire content of the conditioned mind. It is the raw material from which the self is continuously assembled.

The edge of the known is where thought ends and direct perception begins. It is the point at which understanding has taken you as far as understanding can go—and something else is required.

The structure has now been seen.

But seeing the structure is not the end of the journey.

You are standing at that edge now.

Part Two begins on the other side of it.

PART TWO

Seeing the Mechanism

CHAPTER 6

The Gap Between Knowing and Seeing

You've read every book on swimming.

*You understand buoyancy, propulsion,
and breathing technique.*

*You can explain it perfectly—the physics,
the mechanics, the theory.*

Then someone pushes you into the pool.

And you're drowning.

STANDING AT THE EDGE

You can know conceptually that the self is repetitive thought and still be completely identified with every thought that arises. You can understand that the loop reinforces itself and still find yourself trapped inside it day after day. You can believe, philosophically, that awareness exists beyond the loop—and still have no direct experience of it whatsoever.

Intellectual understanding is still thinking. Conceptualizing is thinking. Believing is thinking. Explaining is thinking. Introspecting is thinking. Thought can describe the loop with extraordinary accuracy and remain entirely inside it.

This is the gap that almost every approach to psychological freedom misses—and it is the reason intelligent, sincere, hardworking people can spend years in genuine inquiry and still feel fundamentally unchanged.

Consider someone who has practiced mindfulness or meditation sincerely for years. They have sat with their breath, observed thoughts arising and passing, and learned to create space between stimulus and response. Their practice is genuine. Their effort is real. And in controlled conditions—on the cushion, in a quiet room, in the absence of pressure—they may achieve a temporary stillness. A sense of calm arrives. Awareness feels accessible. The person feels they are making real progress.

Then a family member says something critical at dinner. Or a colleague takes credit for their work without acknowledgment. Or an old relationship pattern surfaces without warning.

The dam breaks—completely, automatically, as if their years of practice never happened. Their stomachs tighten. Their anger floods in. Their familiar story returns: *I knew this would happen. Nothing ever really changes. I must try harder, be more present, not let things affect me like this.*

Their body was already bracing before their mind registered what occurred.

Their practice contained the trigger rather than ending it.

This is not a failure of the practice or the person. It is a structural fact: technique operates within thought, managing the loop's output without touching its source. Knowing operates in thought, which is inside the loop. No amount of thinking can step outside thinking. No accumulation of conceptual insight can observe itself from within the system that generated it.

What changes the relationship to suffering is not more practice nor more understanding, but a shift in how understanding functions—from thought managing the mechanism to awareness perceiving it directly, at the moment it arises, without interference.

This is the movement from knowing to seeing.

THE MOMENT THAT REVEALS THE GAP

Your manager looks at your report and says, "This needs significant improvement."

Instantly, thoughts fire: *I'm such a loser. I always mess up. They probably think I'm incompetent. I knew I shouldn't have volunteered for this project.* The body responds immediately—chest tightens, heat rises in the face, stomach knots, and shoulders tense. The self identifies completely: *I am inadequate. I am a failure.*

In that moment, all understanding vanishes. Not because it was forgotten, but because knowledge is not the same as perception. The knowledge exists as memory. It is available when the system is calm, when there is no threat to identity, when the loop has not yet activated. But when identity feels threatened, and emotion rises, the loop captures attention entirely.

The thought is not recognized as automatic nor is the self recognized as a process. The loop completing itself goes entirely unnoticed. There is only the inside of it—the thoughts, the shame, the inadequacy—experienced as simple reality rather than as a mechanism in motion.

This is what happens when understanding exists only as knowledge: it functions in stable conditions and stands aside when the loop activates. Identification with old beliefs returns as if nothing had ever been understood, because in the moment of activation, the knowledge is simply not where the understanding needs to be.

SEEING AS A CHANGE IN RELATIONSHIPS

Now let's view the same moment but with a different outcome.

Your manager says, "This needs significant improvement." Thought still fires: *Oh, no. I failed.* The body still responds—tension, heat, contraction. The machinery is still machinery. Nothing about the mechanism has changed.

But something is different.

The movement is visible to you. You notice your thought as thought rather than as truth. The bodily response is felt as sensation rather than as proof. The self's attempt to claim the moment—to make it mean something about who you are—is seen as part of the pattern, not followed as instruction.

The thought is not taken as a verdict. The sensation is not taken as evidence. The identification is not pursued.

This does not produce relief. It produces clarity. And from that clarity, reaction no longer carries the same momentum—not because it has been stopped, but because it is no longer operating invisibly. The loop will still complete. Tension may remain in the body. But the quality of the relationship to what is happening has shifted entirely. What was experienced as reality is now seen as a process.

This is the difference between knowing and seeing.

Knowing exists in memory and is available under calm conditions. Seeing happens at the moment thought arises—direct perception of the loop as it unfolds, without interference, without effort, without anyone managing the process.

Seeing cannot be willed into existence. It cannot be practiced as a method. The one who would attempt that practice is thought—the self continuing its movement under a different name, toward a new goal it calls presence or awareness.

THE BECOMING BENEATH THE SEEKING

There is something worth naming directly here, because it is easy to overlook—and it is the root of why the gap between knowing and seeing is so persistent.

Every attempt to get from knowing to seeing is itself a movement of becoming.

I know about the loop; therefore, I need to learn to see it. I understand the mechanism intellectually; therefore, I must now develop direct perception. I am not yet where I need to be; therefore, I must become the kind of person who sees clearly.

The structure is identical to every other project the self has undertaken. The content is different—now it involves awareness and insight rather than confidence or success—but the movement is the same: rejection of what is present, projection of an improved version, effort to close the gap between them.

This same movement is becoming organized around spiritual progress. And becoming, as Part One established, is the self's primary mechanism for sustaining itself. The self seeking to end the self is still the self. The becoming seeking to end becoming is still becoming.

Seeing this, clearly, without judgment—without making it into another problem to solve—is itself the beginning of the shift. Because when the seeking is recognized as seeking, when the becoming is seen as becoming, when the project of trying to get somewhere is observed as just another movement of the conditioned mind—something relaxes that effort.

The gap between knowing and seeing does not close through effort. It closes when effort is seen as unnecessary.

THE STRUCTURAL LIMITS OF INTELLECTUAL CHANGE

Change can occur at many levels. Circumstances can be altered. Behavior can be adjusted. Skills can be acquired. Knowledge can accumulate over the years. All of this is real and valuable—and all of it leaves the deeper structure untouched.

Suffering is not generated at the level of knowledge. It is generated at the level of identity—through conclusions that operate silently, beneath conscious awareness, filtering every experience through the sense of "*I am.*"

You can understand the loop completely and still believe "I am anxious" when anxiety arises. You can explain conditioning with precision and still identify as the kind of person who struggles with this. You can articulate the nature of awareness and still experience every moment from inside the self.

Consider someone who has spent years learning about psychology—studying, analyzing, tracing every pattern back to its origin. They can name every cognitive distortion. They can explain exactly why they react the way they do. And then someone criticizes them and their reaction fires—defensive, wounded, certain of its own justification—as if none of that understanding existed.

Knowledge reorganizes thought. It does not dissolve identification.

Direct perception operates differently. Seeing does not add information to the system. It removes a specific confusion— the confusion that fuses the observer with what is observed, the awareness with the content of awareness. When identification loosens, even briefly, something reorganizes on its own—not through effort, but through the simple clarity of seeing what is actually happening.

But this does not happen through understanding alone. It happens through seeing.

THINKING ABOUT THE LOOP VS. SEEING IT

The difference between these two is subtle but decisive.

Someone says something unkind.

When thinking about the loop, thought immediately engages: *I know this pattern. I shouldn't react. My conditioning is firing. My body is responding. Why can't I stop this?* The loop continues—now with a self-aware supervisor installed. The self has simply added another layer: the one who knows about the loop, watches the loop, and tries to manage it from a slightly superior perspective.

The knowledge is real. The supervision is sincere. The loop is still running, and the self is still its center.

When seeing the loop, something different is operating. There is no supervisor. There is just attention—open, without agenda, not trying to change what is noticed or improve the outcome. Thought arises. Sensation forms. The movement completes itself without interference from a self trying to manage it.

The unkind comment is registered. The thought is seen as thought. The sensation is felt as sensation. Nothing is added to or subtracted from what is actually happening.

What changes is not the content of experience but the relationship to it. The comment does not go unnoticed. The thought does not stop arising. But without identification, the movement loses its grip as it pulls the loop tighter and tighter. What was personal becomes observable. What felt like reality is seen as a process.

The loop does not end through effort. It loses momentum when it is no longer fed by identification.

WHY THE SELF CAN'T SEE ITSELF

The self instinctively tries to turn seeing into a project. This is not a failure. It is simply what the self does with everything it encounters.

Reading this, your thought may already be firing: *I need to see more clearly. I should practice direct perception. I will pay more attention to the loop.* The intention feels genuine. The motivation feels correct.

But who is this "I" who will now practice seeing? It is the self. It is the movement of thoughts. It is the loop continuing under a new name—this time called awareness practice, or presence work, or consciousness development.

An eye cannot see itself. A knife cannot cut itself. Thought cannot observe thought from a position outside thought. When thought attempts to watch itself as a method, it is still thought watching thought. That strengthens the observer—and the observer is still the self.

This is why so many sincere practices fail to produce lasting transformation. They create a spiritual self—the one who is aware, the one who is watching, the one who is diligently developing consciousness—while leaving the underlying structure entirely intact. The content changes. The identity shifts from *I am anxious* to *I am someone observing my anxiety*. The loop continues under a more respectable name.

Seeing is not something the self does.

Seeing happens when the self is absent.

EFFORT, CONCENTRATION, AND AWARENESS

There is a distinction here that is easy to miss—and missing it leads to years of misdirected practice.

Concentration is effortful. It narrows attention onto a specific object, excludes everything else, and requires energy to sustain. When concentration ends, the narrowing ends with it. This is why focus achieved through effort cannot be maintained indefinitely—it requires constant input from the very self it is trying to transcend.

Awareness is not concentration. It is not created through effort or sustained through will. Seeing is open, inclusive, effortless—not a beam directed at experience, but the space in which experience appears. It is not something generated by practice. It is what remains when the self-directed effort ends.

When someone sits to meditate and tries hard to be aware—watching thoughts, catching distractions, returning attention to the breath—that effort is still the self doing something. The trying is the self. The returning is the self. The monitoring of whether it is working is the self.

Awareness itself requires none of this. It is already present. It is not behind the effort—it is what the effort is obscuring.

What obscures awareness is always the same thing: identification with the self, which claims experience as mine, the loop running automatically and interpreting everything through the lens of me. When the loop is seen clearly—not controlled, not fought, not improved—awareness is simply what remains.

> *Right now, without doing anything, notice: is there awareness present? Not awareness of something in particular—just the simple fact of being aware. You did not produce this. It was already here before you looked for it. The effort to find awareness is itself happening inside awareness. Awareness was always present, obscured not by distance but by occupation.*

WHAT SEEING ACTUALLY IS

Seeing is direct perception without the filter of thought.

Look at something in the external world right now—whatever is nearby. Thought labels it almost immediately: chair, window, plant, wall. Then the thought continues: *I need to clean that. I remember when I bought it; that color doesn't work with the rest of the room.* Within seconds, direct perception has been replaced by memory, association, and evaluation. The thing itself has receded behind the commentary.

But in the fraction of a second before the label arrived, there was just seeing. Color. Shape. Light. Direct contact with what is there, before thought arrived to tell you what it is and what it means.

The same movement appears inwardly.

Anxiety arises and thought labels it immediately: *I am anxious.* More thoughts follow: *Why am I anxious? I shouldn't be. What's wrong with me? I need to fix this.* The loop intensifies through identification and resistance. Each thought adds another layer.

In seeing, something different happens. There is tightness in the chest. Heat in the face. Contraction in the throat. There may even be a thought saying *I am anxious.* But the thought remains a thought. The sensation remains sensation. Nothing is denied, and nothing is made personal. No story is built around it, and no project is created to resolve it.

This is the loop seen in action—directly, without interference.

And when the loop is seen this way, it loses its authority over behavior.

WHAT ACTUALLY CHANGES

Seeing does not stop thought from arising. The brain still references memory. The body still responds to signals. The machinery still runs.

What changes is one's relationship to the mechanism.

When the loop runs without being seen, *I am anxious* feels like identity—a fact about who you are, permanent, personal, and demanding a response. The sensation is taken as proof. The thought is taken as truth. Anxiety and I are fused into a single experience that must now be managed, escaped, or overcome.

When the loop is seen, something shifts. Anxiety is recognized as sensation plus thought—conditioning in motion, the body executing a signal, interpretation running from memory. The pattern is observable rather than invisible. What was experienced as reality is now visible as a process. The thought is still there. The sensation is still there. But the fusion has loosened.

The content may still appear. The loop may still complete. But identification weakens—and in that weakening, there is space. In that space, something other than automatic reaction becomes possible. A response can emerge that is not simply the loop continuing under a slightly different shape.

This is freedom—not freedom from sensation or thought, but freedom from being entirely captured and driven by them.

WHY READING ISN'T SWIMMING

The pool is still there.

The theory was accurate. The mechanics were correct. The understanding was genuine.

But when you hit the water, you started to drown.

Reading about water is not being in it. Understanding the loop is not seeing it. Knowing the mechanism exists does not interrupt identification at the moment it tightens around something real.

The gap between knowing and seeing is not a failure of intelligence. It is not insufficient effort or a lack of sincerity. It is simply the nature of the territory—and recognizing this gap clearly, without self-judgment, is itself the beginning of something different.

The question is no longer: *how do I better understand this?*

The question is: *what is actually happening right now, in this moment, as I read these words?*

Understanding the mechanism does not end the loop. Seeing it directly does.

Notice this moment. Not the ideas on these pages—the actual experience of reading. There are words on a page. There is the act of reading. There is a thought arising to interpret what is being read. There is, somewhere in the background, something aware of all of it. Where are you in this? Are you the thoughts arising? Are you the awareness in which they appear? Just look—not to answer correctly, but to see what is actually here.

CHAPTER 7

What Blocks Direct Perception

It's drizzling outside.

You sit by the window with your favorite cup of tea, journal open.

The room is quiet.
The moment is settled.

A sound breaks your focus.
You glance up.

A speck on the glass catches your eye.
"Need to clean that later."

The thought is quick and efficient.
You return to your journal.

You looked. But you didn't see.

Birds were dancing on the branches, inches from your window.

WHAT BLOCKS SEEING

Seeing is immediate. Awareness is always in the present. And yet direct perception feels rare—often unavailable precisely when it is most needed, in the moments of pressure, conflict, and strong emotion when it would matter most.

The primary block is not a distraction or lack of discipline. It is thought itself—not as a problem to be solved, but as a quality that makes direct perception structurally difficult.

Thought is *exclusive*. It narrows attention through judgment, comparison, naming, and interpretation. It pulls attention inward—toward what this means, how it relates to me, what should happen next, what went wrong before. Thought is always moving from the present toward relevance, implication, and personal meaning.

Awareness, by contrast, is *inclusive*. It does not select, judge, or compare. It does not narrow attention toward what matters to the self. It opens—allowing everything to be as it is, without privileging one fragment of experience over another.

One is partial. The other is whole.

Consider a conversation where something difficult is said. Thought immediately engages: *Was that a criticism? What did they mean? How should I respond? What does this say about how they see me?* In that inward movement, the actual person sitting across from you recedes. Their tone, their expression, the quality of what is happening between you—all of it disappears behind the internal activity of your thinking about it. You are present in body. Your attention is elsewhere entirely.

When thought dominates attention, awareness is not blocked by force—it is crowded out. Attention is consumed by thinking, leaving no space for direct perception of what is actually happening. This is why even subtle, quiet thoughts can prevent seeing. They do not need to be loud or dramatic. They need only to occupy your attention.

Seeing requires space. Thought consumes space.

WHAT THOUGHT DOES TO EXPERIENCE

Without understanding this dynamic, life is lived almost entirely within the field of thought. And because thought is limited—constrained by memory, conditioning, and experience—the entire experience of reality becomes limited in the same way.

Thought divides. It creates *me and not-me, a right and a wrong, a past and a future, a here and a somewhere better.* This division produces inner conflict. Conflict consumes energy. A mind in conflict cannot see clearly, because the energy required for clear perception is being spent on the internal war.

Consider a familiar moment: someone needs to make an important decision. Their thinking is relentless. Every option generates counterarguments. Every possibility generates fear of the alternative. The mind circles, weighs, and compares—and the more it thinks, the less clear the decision becomes. Not because the choice is genuinely impossible, but because thought is consuming the very clarity that would allow the choice to be seen.

When thought quiets—not through suppression or force, but through being seen—something opens on its own. Energy spent on internal conflict becomes available. Decisions that felt impossibly heavy simplify. Action becomes direct rather than reactive because it is no longer filtered through the accumulated anxiety of a self trying to protect itself.

What emerges is not confidence built from past success—another product of memory. It is trust that arises from seeing clearly what is actually happening in this moment, without the overlay of accumulated conclusions.

WHEN THE OBSERVER DISAPPEARS

When you try to watch your thoughts, who is watching?

This question is not philosophical; it's sincere.

Thought watching thought. The self observing the self. This creates a division that feels natural—there appears to be an observer standing separate from what is observed, a me that is aware of thoughts, emotions, and patterns. The division seems obvious. It does not withstand careful examination.

The observer is also thought. The one who claims to watch is the same movement of conditioning it claims to be observing.

When you say I am observing my anxiety, the I doing the observing is itself the self—formed through repetition, sustained by identification, made of the same material as what it claims to be watching.

The observer is not separate from conditioning. It is conditioning observing itself and calling that observation awareness.

This is why many meditation and mindfulness techniques, practiced sincerely over the years, fail to produce the lasting transformation they promise. They strengthen the observer. They refine the self into a more vigilant, more disciplined, more apparently aware version of itself. The content shifts from gross suffering to subtle monitoring. The structure remains intact.

Consider what actually happens in the moment the division collapses—not as a concept, but as a lived experience. There is tightness in the chest. There is no one standing apart from it, analyzing it, trying to understand its origin or manage its expression. There is simply the sensation of tightness without a story around it, experience without an experiencer standing outside it claiming ownership. In that moment, something is seen that cannot be seen while the observer is present.

True seeing occurs when the division collapses—when thought is simply seen as thought, sensation felt as sensation, with no one positioned above the experience trying to improve, control, or escape what is happening.

This is not a practice. It is a recognition. And recognition cannot be manufactured—it can only be noticed when it occurs.

WHY DOES EFFORT PREVENT SEEING

Effort is a subtle yet powerful obstruction—and it is easy to miss because it feels like the appropriate response to a problem.

When something is not working, the instinct is to try harder. This works perfectly in the world of technical skills, but not so much in psychology. When awareness seems absent, the response is to focus more intently. When the loop keeps running, the impulse is to apply more discipline. This instinct is sincere. It is also the self continuing its movement, using the tools it knows, toward a destination that effort cannot reach.

The language of effort reveals the structure beneath it: *I must be more aware. I should pay attention. I need to catch thoughts earlier.* Each of these statements reinforces precisely what it seeks to transcend—a self that is not yet adequate, working toward something it does not yet have, measuring its progress against a standard it has imposed on itself.

Effort creates tension. Tension occupies attention. Occupied attention consumes mental space. A mind with no space cannot see clearly.

Consider what happens when someone sits to meditate, seeking a quiet mind. The seeking itself becomes the problem. Every thought that arises is evaluated: *Is this the kind of thought I should be having?* Every distraction is caught and returned. Every moment of quiet is monitored to see whether it is deepening or dissolving. The mind is working extraordinarily hard. And all that work is the very noise it is trying to silence.

When you try to be aware, attention moves into the trying. The effort becomes the content. The hunter and the hunted are the same movement.

Seeing happens when effort relaxes—not through collapse or indifference, but through understanding so complete that effort is seen as unnecessary. When the observer is recognized as the observed, who remains to make the effort? When identification is seen as the source of the confusion, what is there to do?

THE SUBTLE TRAP OF SPIRITUAL IDENTITY

After genuine moments of direct perception, thought often returns quickly, claiming the experience.

I was aware. I finally saw it. I'm becoming more conscious. Something is shifting in me.

A new identity forms quietly—the one who experienced clarity, the one who is developing presence, the one who now understands how the loop works. The content has changed entirely, but the structure has not moved. Identification has simply shifted its object from suffering to insight.

This is extraordinarily easy to miss precisely because it feels like progress—and because it produces a genuine sense of meaning and direction, pushing the self to continue functioning as a self.

Consider what happens after a genuine moment of seeing. Something was clear—the loop visible, thought recognized as thought, sensation felt without story. Then, within moments: *That was it. That's what's being described. I need to remember how that felt so I can return to it. I should tell someone about this. I wonder if this is what awakening feels like.*

The seeking has resumed. The self has reclaimed the territory. Now there is a new goal—*more of that, please*—and the spiritual project has a fresh supply of fuel.

The spiritual self is the ordinary self wearing different clothing. It has the same structure, the same movement of becoming, the same need to measure itself, protect its gains, and secure its position. Only the vocabulary has changed.

Awareness has no identity. There is no I in seeing. When perception is genuinely direct, there is only perception—no one claiming ownership, no one filing the experience away for later use or comparison. The moment thought says *I am aware,* awareness has already been replaced by self-reference.

This does not mean something has gone wrong. It means thought has resumed its natural activity. The problem arises only when this movement is not seen for what it is.

THE ILLUSION OF PROGRESS

Progress exists in psychological time. It requires a before and an after—a self that was less advanced, working toward a self that is more advanced. It requires measurement, comparison, and a destination.

Seeing does not accumulate. Awareness cannot be stockpiled. There is no gradual arrival at direct perception. Either there is seeing in this moment—or there isn't. The previous moments of clarity do not transfer to the current one. Each moment is complete in itself, or it is not.

Something real does shift over time. Identification may loosen more quickly after being activated. Recovery from strong emotional reactions may happen faster. Thought may be recognized earlier in its movement. These are genuine changes—and the moment they are interpreted as spiritual progress, the self has returned, measuring, comparing, tracking its own development.

Consider what happens when someone believes they have made significant spiritual progress. They handle a difficult conversation with unusual clarity. They notice the loop firing without reacting. They feel genuinely more settled and open. Then something unexpected arrives—a sudden loss, an old wound reopened, a relationship under acute pressure—and their reaction is as automatic as it ever was. The apparent years of progress dissolve in a moment.

This is not a failure. It is the nature of the territory.

What shifts is the speed with which thought is recognized as thought—the gap between activation and recognition narrows. But this is not the self improving itself. It is understanding deepening—and intellectual understanding, as this entire section has explored, is not the same as seeing.

The moment progress is claimed, the self has returned and is measuring itself again.

WHY METHODS FAIL

The mind, faced with this territory, naturally reaches for a method. The reaching is sincere. But methods belong to becoming—they assume a self that is not yet where it needs to be, assigning it a role in getting there. Any technique aimed at producing seeing is still the self moving toward something. And that movement is precisely what needs to stop for seeing to occur.

What is needed is not a new technique. It is a different quality of attention—one that is not directed anywhere, not trying to achieve a result. When attention rests without an agenda and without the self measuring its performance, something is already possible that no method can manufacture.

Seeing happens when effort relaxes. Not when it is applied more precisely.

PERCEPTION WITHOUT INTERFERENCE

Seeing is not mystical. It is not extraordinary or elevated or reserved for the spiritually advanced.

It is the most ordinary thing possible—perception without interference.

When you perceive something in the world before naming it, that is seeing. When you notice a sensation without immediately converting it into *my anxiety* or *my excitement*, that is seeing. When a thought appears, and you recognize it as a thought—without following it, without adding a story, without trying to make it stop—that is seeing.

None of this requires special conditions. Seeing does not require a new belief, a prepared state, the absence of difficulty, or years of practice. It can happen in the middle of a difficult conversation, in the presence of strong emotion, in the completely unremarkable texture of an ordinary day.

What makes it rare is not its difficulty. What makes it rare is that attention is almost always occupied—by thought, by meaning-making, by the self's continuous commentary on what is happening and what it means and what should be done next.

When that occupation loosens—even briefly, even accidentally—perception is simply what remains. Not a special kind of perception. Nothing elevated or refined. Just what is actually here without the overlay of conclusion and story layered on top of it.

In seeing, nothing is excluded. Sensations are present. Emotions move. But there is no compulsion to follow any of it, no demand that it be different, no urgency to convert the experience into evidence about who you are.

This is what was always available. It was never absent. It was simply overlooked—by attention that was elsewhere, occupied by the known.

A NEW RELATIONSHIP

Seeing does not eliminate thought completely. The brain continues to function. The body continues to respond. Memories surface when triggered. The machinery continues exactly as before.

What changes is the relationship to the mechanism, to the self.

Before seeing, *I am anxious* feels like identity—a fact about who you are, permanent and personal, demanding a response. The sensation is proof. The thought is truth. *Anxiety* and *I* are fused into a single experience that must now be managed.

After seeing, anxiety is an experience—nothing more than that. Sensation is sensation. Thought is thought. *I am anxious* becomes *I feel anxious*. And I feel anxious is recognized as an old pattern repeating, not as a verdict being delivered about something permanent.

This shift is not dramatic when it occurs. It does not announce itself with ceremony. Consider a familiar moment of conflict—someone dismisses something you've said, and your familiar feeling of contraction arises. Heat in the face, tightening in the chest, the thought: *they never take me seriously*. In the past, that thought would have been the beginning of a long story—rehearsed grievances, defensive preparation, hours of internal argument about what was said and what it meant.

With seeing, the thought is noticed as thought. The sensation is felt as sensation. The story is seen before it is entered—not suppressed, not analyzed, not replaced with a better story. Simply visible. And in being visible, it does not have the same grip.

The content remains. The relationship has changed. And that change, quiet as it is, is the thing that matters.

WHY YOU MISSED THE BIRDS

You looked at the window. Light entered your eyes. The scene was fully present—rain, branches, birds dancing inches away from where you sat.

But your attention landed on the speck. Your thought narrowed around it: *need to clean that later*. In that narrowing, the rest of the scene receded. Not because it was hidden, but because attention was fully occupied by something else.

The birds were always there.

Thought did not block your seeing by force. Your vision was blocked by thought's occupation. And the one who might have tried harder to see the birds would also have been thought—another movement of the same mechanism, looking for what was already standing in front of it.

When occupation loosens, nothing special needs to be added. The scene was never incomplete. The awareness required to see it was never absent.

The birds were never hidden. They were simply overlooked.

> *In this moment—not as a practice, just as honest observation—is there anything occupying attention right now besides what is actually here? Some background commentary, some evaluation of what you've read, some flicker of something unresolved from earlier in the day? Just notice what is present. Not to clear it away. Simply to see that your attention is occupied and to observe what is doing the occupying.*

CHAPTER 8

The Conditioning We Carry

The old record spins.

The same song.

The same notes.

The same rhythm.

Not because the record chooses.

Because the grooves were cut that way.

The needle follows the path already carved.

It has no choice.

THE FILTER YOU DIDN'T CHOOSE

Conditioning is not an abstract psychological concept. It is the structure through which reality is filtered—moment by moment, automatically, beneath the level at which conscious choice operates.

Your conditioning shapes what you notice in a room before you have decided what to look for. It determines how a tone of voice lands in your body before you have processed the words. It generates a sense of threat or safety in response to the most ordinary situations—a look, a pause in a conversation, the way someone's shoulders are held—before any thinking has occurred.

You walk into a room full of strangers and immediately feel self-conscious. Someone criticizes your work, and a feeling of inadequacy floods in before you have evaluated whether the criticism is valid. A compliment arrives, and you deflect it automatically, without deciding to. These are not random reactions, nor are they character flaws. They are grooves cut long ago, playing automatically, without asking permission.

The record spins. The needle follows. And most of the time, you might not notice this is happening—because it is not you choosing, but conditioning executing.

WHAT DOES CONDITIONING MEAN IN DAILY LIFE

The most important thing to understand about conditioning is that two people can witness the same external event and have completely different internal experiences—not because one is stronger or more evolved, but because their conditioning is different.

Two people witness a manager publicly criticizing an employee.

One person, whose early experience of authority was harsh and unpredictable, immediately feels anxiety flood in. Thought fires: *This could be me next time. I need to stay invisible. I must not be heard or seen.* The body tightens. Identity feels threatened.

Another person, whose experience of authority was mostly supportive, witnesses the same scene and responds differently. Their thoughts tell them: *That manager lacks communication skills. Poor feedback damages morale.* That person's body remains calm, as they are experiencing no threat to their identity.

Same event. Completely different internal experience.

This is conditioning in action—not as theory, but as the lived mechanism that determines what you notice, how you interpret it, what it means to your body, and how you respond. Conditioning operates automatically, instantly, before any conscious choice has been made.

PSYCHOLOGICAL CONDITIONING: WHERE SUFFERING ORIGINATES

Not all conditioning operates at the same level, and it is worth being precise about this—because freedom does not come from opposing what cannot be changed.

Biological responses are not psychological conditioning. When the body is deprived of sleep, food, or safety, functioning degrades. When a threat is present, the nervous system activates. These are hard-wired survival responses. They can be understood and worked with intelligently, but they cannot be transcended through insight. The person who has not slept in three days and feels irritable does not have a conditioning problem. They need rest.

Genetic temperament is similarly not psychological conditioning. Some nervous systems are more sensitive than others. Some people process sensory input more intensely, recover more slowly from stress, or are more reactive by structural disposition. Understanding this removes unnecessary self-blame and allows genuine accommodation rather than a constant battle with one's own biology.

Psychological conditioning is where suffering originates— and it is the only layer that can be seen through. This layer consists of beliefs, emotional patterns, habitual reactions, interpretive filters, and self-image. Unlike biology and genetics, your psychological conditioning is not hard-wired. You learned it through experience, repetition, and the early construction of identity described in Chapter 4. And what is learned can be seen. And what is seen can no longer operate with the same invisible authority.

HOW PSYCHOLOGICAL CONDITIONING FORMS

Psychological conditioning follows a predictable sequence—and understanding that sequence matters, because it shows exactly where the mechanism can be interrupted.

The formation of your psychological conditioning begins with **information**: what you are repeatedly exposed to—words, behaviors, emotional environments, cultural messages, the implicit rules of the household you grew up in. A child hears, again and again: *You need to be careful. You need to work hard and prove your worth. The world is a dangerous place. Don't trust anyone. You are nothing until you are somebody or something.* These are not neutral pieces of information, as they carry emotional weight from the people delivering them.

Then comes **attention**—the repeated replaying of the message, the emotional investment that reinforces it. The child doesn't hear the warning once. Those warnings return in moments of uncertainty, in the parent's worried face before the child tries something new, in the anxiety transmitted through a thousand small moments that say: *your worth is determined by the* *approval of others.* The emotional weight deepens the neural pathway. The message starts to feel true. By adolescence, the thought arises automatically, without the need for an external voice: *I should try harder. I must become better. I need to improve myself.* The voice has been internalized.

Eventually, the pattern becomes condition—automatic, unconscious, self-executing. By adulthood, new opportunities are dismissed before they are fully considered. The hesitation is not experienced as a decision, but as a simple fact about how things are. Reaction precedes awareness entirely.

This is why willpower so consistently fails. Most attempts at change begin after one's conditioning has already been executed. You notice the hesitation, the withdrawal, the familiar self-doubt—but the conditioning has already run. Trying to override it from that point is like trying to catch a train that has already left.

The shift that actually matters happens earlier—not through control, but through seeing.

When the thought *I shouldn't try* is recognized as conditioning—as an old pattern repeating from a time and a context that may have nothing to do with the present— something shifts. The groove does not disappear. But it no longer operates invisibly. And in its visibility, something other than automatic execution becomes possible.

SELF-IMAGE AS THE DEEPEST GROOVE

Self-image is the most powerful form of psychological conditioning because it does not merely shape individual reactions—it determines what feels possible before anything is even attempted.

How you feel about yourself is not just a belief among other beliefs. It is the lens through which all beliefs are formed. Your self-image is the filter through which every experience, every piece of feedback, every success, and every failure is processed and assigned meaning.

Consider the same situation, entered with two different self-images.

A person whose self-image is organized around *I am capable* receives critical feedback. Their thought interprets: *This is useful information. I can adjust and improve.* The feedback is processed, their behavior adapts, and that person moves forward without their identity being threatened.

A person whose self-image is organized around *I am inadequate* receives the same feedback from the same person in the same words. Their thought interprets: *This confirms what I already knew. I'm not good enough.* The feedback becomes proof—not of the specific mistake, but of the fundamental inadequacy that was already assumed. Their identity is threatened, and their withdrawal begins. They hide themselves and wish to be invisible.

Same words. Completely different experience. Because the same external event has been processed through two entirely different internal structures.

Freedom does not come from replacing a negative self-image with a positive one—that is still conditioning, just oriented differently. Real psychological freedom comes from seeing the mechanism of self-image itself: watching how it filters, shapes interpretation, and converts neutral events into evidence for predetermined conclusions. When self-image is seen as conditioning rather than as truth, its authority over experience weakens—not through effort, but through recognition.

CONDITIONING AND THE KNOWN

All psychological conditioning operates within the known—within the accumulated field of memory, interpretation, belief, and prior conclusion.

The known is the past operating in the present. When you meet someone new, thought references the known immediately: *They remind me of someone. I trust people like this. I've been hurt by people like this before.* Before any real contact has occurred, interpretation has already filtered the encounter. The person in front of you is being seen through the lens of everyone who came before them.

The unknown is not mysterious or elevated. It is simply experience that has not yet been filtered through memory—direct contact with what is actually present, before the known moves in to categorize and conclude.

The known is necessary. Without it, you could not navigate the world—could not use language, recognize faces, learn from experience, protect yourself from harm, or function in any practical sense. The question is not whether the known is present, guiding your behaviors and reactions. The question is whether the known dominates your perception entirely, converting every new experience into a variation of an old one, and every new person into a character from a previous chapter.

When conditioning is seen clearly—when the known is recognized as the known, rather than mistaken for the simply real—something opens. The past no longer fills every available mental space. And in that open space, direct contact with what is actually here becomes possible.

THE WEIGHT OF LIVING FROM THE KNOWN

There is a felt quality to living entirely from accumulated conditioning—a particular heaviness that is so constant it often goes unnoticed until it lifts.

A feeling of obligation arises from maintaining identity. We feel burdened from carrying the past into every present moment. We find ourselves constantly seeking because of the incompleteness built into becoming. Our discontent is structural—not a response to circumstances, but a consequence of living in the gap between what is and what the self tells us it is.

Consider the feeling of obligation. An invitation arrives, and immediately there is pressure: *I really don't want to go anywhere, but I should go. What will they think if I don't? I don't want to let them down.* The response is not to the event itself but to the self-image being maintained: *I am the kind of person who shows up, who is reliable, who does not disappoint.* The event has not happened yet, but the weight of identity defending itself is already present.

When these states arise—obligation, burden, seeking, discontent—they are not personal failures. They are structural indicators. They are the felt experience of your active conditioning dominating your perception.

When this is seen, when *"I should go"* is recognized as conditioning protecting a self-image rather than as a simple truth about what is needed—the pressure changes. Recognizing your conditioning doesn't mean you'll ignore the pressure, only see it clearly. Your response may even be the same. You may still attend. But your internal relationship to the invitation has shifted. The weight is different when you can see it as weight, rather than experience the pressure you put on yourself as simply how things are and must always be.

SEEING CONDITIONING WITHOUT JUDGEMENT

Judging conditioning is itself conditioning.

When patterns are judged—*I shouldn't still be reacting this way. What's wrong with me? I know better than this*—the conditioned self is using conditioning to evaluate itself, generating a second layer of suffering on top of the first. The pattern continues, now wearing the additional label of self-improvement in progress.

Seeing without judgment is of a different quality. Direct perception is simple, direct observation—without resistance, without correction, without attachment, without a personal interpretation projected toward what is noticed.

You receive criticism. Defensiveness arises immediately. Your thought fires: *They're wrong. They don't understand. I need to explain myself.*

When you add judgment of your defensiveness: *I shouldn't be defensive. I know better than this. Why can't I just receive feedback calmly?* Now there are two layers: defensiveness and the judgment of defensiveness. The loop intensifies. The self is at war with itself.

Without judgment: There is still the feeling of defensiveness. The body is still tight. Thought is still preparing to defend. But there's a space before you react, and in that space, you see through this whole movement. You offer no resistance, no correction, no attachment. You don't launch a project to fix anything. You are instead able to make a clear observation of what is present.

Though defensiveness may still be there, you are able to see it as conditioning in motion—not as a personal failure, not as evidence of your inadequacy, just as a pattern executing. And in that seeing, without the added energy of judgment and resistance, your reactivity does not deepen in the same way. What is seen clearly tends to lose its compulsion, not because it is controlled, but because your identification has dissolved. You are watching the pattern rather than being it.

The difference is subtle. The consequences are not.

THE GROOVES THAT PLAY YOU

The record does not choose the song.

The grooves were carved through repetition—through the accumulated experiences of a lifetime, beginning long before you had the capacity to evaluate or question anything. The needle follows the path already cut, and it has no agency in the matter.

This is conditioning. Not a moral failure. Not weakness. Not something to be ashamed of nor urgently fixed. Just structure— the structure of a mind that has been learning and storing and responding since long before consciousness was capable of watching it do so.

You cannot erase the grooves. They are neural pathways, a physical structure, laid down through years of repetition. But when they are seen operating—when the needle is observed following the groove rather than the observation arriving after the song has already been played—they no longer play entirely unnoticed.

The record may still spin. The song may still exist.

But you were never the song. You were always the awareness in which the song plays.

And that distinction, once genuinely seen, changes everything about what the music is able to do.

> *Think of a conditioning pattern you recognize in yourself—a reaction that fires reliably in certain situations, a self-image that shapes what feels possible. Don't try to change it. Don't analyze its origin. Just observe it, as directly as you can, as it is right now. Is there a way in which you have been the song, believing yourself to be the record, the needle, and the groove all at once? What would it mean to simply just watch, without resistance, without a project attached to the watching?*

CHAPTER 9

Seeing in Daily Life

The lake is still.

No wind ripples the water.

You see the mountain clearly, mirrored in the lake's surface.

Then someone throws a stone into the water.

Ripples spread. The reflection fragments.

You watch.

The ripples pass.

The water settles.

The mountain appears again—undistorted.

WHAT THIS LOOKS LIKE WHEN IT'S REAL

The ripples pass. The water settles. Clarity returns.

But what does that mean in lived experience—not as poetic description, but as the actual texture of daily life?

Seeing is not a permanent state that, once reached, never leaves. Seeing is not a spiritual achievement that removes you from the ordinary difficulties of being human. Seeing happens in moments—when your thoughts quiet, when your identification loosens, when you recognize your conditioning in the instant before it fully executes.

The question is not whether these moments occur. They do, in every person, more often than is usually recognized. The question is: what is different when you are having these seeing moments?

And what does the territory look like when seeing is present—not occasionally or in retreat conditions, but in the unremarkable movement of an ordinary day?

WHAT DOES *NOT* HAPPEN

Before describing what changes, it helps to be precise about what does not change—because expectations can quietly become another form of becoming.

When conditioning is seen clearly, you do not transcend humanity. You do not escape emotion, live in perpetual ease, become immune to pain, stop thinking, or arrive at a permanent state of undisturbed clarity.

Pain continues. Psychological suffering does not—or rather, it does not continue with the same force and the same inevitability.

Pain belongs to life. Loss brings grief. Fatigue is real. A genuine threat produces genuine fear. These are biological and emotional responses to real conditions, and they are not the problem this book is addressing.

Suffering is something else. Suffering is the psychological commentary layered onto experience—the story built on top of the sensation, the meaning added to the event, the identity mobilized to respond to what is happening.

You stub your toe. The pain is immediate, sharp, and undeniable. That is pain, and it is real.

Then thought arrives: *I'm so clumsy. Why can't I pay attention? This is going to hurt all day. I have that meeting later—how am I going to focus?* Now there are two layers: the physical sensation and the psychological elaboration constructed on top of it.

When seeing is present, the toe still throbs. The pain is still there. But the narrative loses momentum. You still feel the sensation. But you also see your inner commentary as just commentary—not as additional reality, not as evidence of something true about who you are. Your experience remains,

but your resistance weakens. And the difference between pain
and psychological suffering is huge.

WHAT ACTUALLY CHANGES

When you are able to see, your reactivity decreases—not
because reactions stop arising, but because there is space
between trigger and response that did not exist before.

Before seeing, your reaction is immediate. Someone
criticizes you and thought fires: *They're wrong about me. I need to
defend myself.* The body tightens. The self feels threatened.
Response is driven by conditioning rather than by what the
situation actually requires.

After seeing, there is a space. The criticism lands. Thought
still arises. The body still responds. The defensive pattern may
still activate. But all of this is visible to you now. And what is
visible loses its compulsion. You may still respond—but the
response comes from clarity rather than from the urgency of
protecting an image.

Your identification loosens. Before seeing, every inner event
is personal: *my anxiety, my failure, my inadequacy, my struggle.* After
seeing, the content remains, but the grip on it changes. Anxiety
may arise, but you can see it as a pattern in motion—not as your
identity, not as the truth about who you are. The thought *not
good enough* appears, but it is recognized as thought—old

conditioning repeating—rather than as a verdict being delivered.

This is not dissociation. You still feel. You still care. You are not watching life from a distance. You are simply no longer consumed by every movement of the conditioned mind.

Old patterns lose their grip. Conditioning does not instantly disappear. Grooves carved over decades do not vanish overnight. But they lose their ability to run entirely unseen. A familiar thought fires—*I always fail at this*—and it is recognized as the groove playing itself, not as reality speaking. When a pattern is clearly seen, it cannot operate with the same hidden authority. The old pattern may still arise. But you are no longer inside it, identifying with it, and believing it as truth.

Psychological time weakens. The self still lives in constant movement between what was and what should be. After seeing this, the movement does not stop entirely, but its urgency diminishes. You still plan. You still learn from experience. You still care about outcomes. But the internal pressure to become someone different—to earn worth, prove value, secure identity against all possible threats—begins to dissolve. Life is met more directly: less through *why does this happen to me*, and more through what is actually happening *for* you.

Clarity replaces confusion. When conditioning runs unconsciously, confusion multiplies: *What should I do? What will people think? What if I make the wrong choice? What if this is already wrong?* When conditioning is seen, choices simplify—not because life becomes simple, but because the inner war is no longer consuming the energy you need to see clearly. You see what the situation requires. You act, or you don't. The war inside you quiets.

WHEN INSIGHT ARRIVES

There is something that needs to be named here directly, because it is the answer to the question Part One raised and left open: *if the self cannot change itself from within, what actually produces the shift?*

The answer is **insight.**

Not insight as a synonym for intellectual understanding— not the accumulation of more information, more clarity about the mechanism, more precise conceptual knowledge about how the loop works. Insight in a more specific and more radical sense: a direct seeing that arrives unbidden, that changes the relationship to something instantly, that does not require effort to produce and cannot be forced into being.

Insight is born out of a new understanding. It usually arises from a sudden realization of how something works, what we usually call an "aha" moment. Insight is not a guarantee; you cannot count on insight arising from sustained practice nor the culmination of years of seeking. Insight is not the guaranteed achievement of someone who has finally done enough work. Insight arrives in the present moment—the only place it can arrive, because it is not a product of thought.

Consider a moment when something you had understood intellectually for years suddenly became simply obvious—when the gap between knowing and seeing closed, not through additional effort but through a quality of attention that was simply present in that moment. Perhaps it happened in the middle of a conversation, or while you were alone in an ordinary room, or in the instant of your waking. The content seen was not new, but your relationship to it had changed entirely. What had been a concept became a direct experience. What had been believed became simply seen.

That is insight. And it cannot be manufactured by the self.

However, the conditions that prevent insight can be recognized:

- The effort that keeps attention occupied.
- The seeking that keeps the mechanism running.
- The becoming that keeps the self in motion, looking for the thing in which it is standing.

When these are seen—not as problems to fix, but as movements of the conditioned mind—they tend to quiet on their own. And in that quieting, something other than the conditioned mind becomes available.

Insight is not something you do. It is something that happens when you stop doing what prevents it.

FREEDOM AS THE ABSENCE OF PSYCHOLOGICAL CONFLICT

Freedom, in the sense this book is discussing, is not the absence of difficulty. Real freedom is the absence of unnecessary psychological struggle in our daily life.

You will still face loss, uncertainty, challenge, and the ordinary pain of being alive in a world that does not arrange itself around your desires. But you will no longer be at war with experience—no longer battling what is happening as if it should not be happening, no longer generating suffering on top of the pain.

In relationships, conflict no longer automatically threatens identity. You can hear something difficult without needing to win the argument immediately. You can be vulnerable without your exposure feeling catastrophic. You can disagree without needing to prove the other person wrong in order for you to feel okay.

Your partner says something critical. Before seeing, thought defends immediately: *They don't understand. They're attacking me. I need to explain why they're wrong.* The conversation becomes a negotiation between two self-protecting systems. After seeing, the criticism is actually heard, not just processed through the filter of how it affects your image. The defensive pattern may still activate, but it's visible. You can pause. You can ask what is actually being said.

At work, feedback no longer collapses you into self-image. Mistakes are acknowledged without spiraling you into a belief in your fundamental inadequacy. Challenges are approached directly rather than avoided to protect a sense of capability that depends on never being tested.

In daily moments, anxiety arises and is seen as a pattern—not as who you are. Thought spins future stories and is recognized as thought—not as prophecy. Sadness moves through without resistance or identity attached to it. Anger arises and passes when it is not fed by the story of who wronged you and why.

Freedom is not what you gain. It is what remains when resistance ends.

THE PARADOX OF TRANSFORMATION

Transformation does not occur because you attempt to transform. Instead, it occurs when what is present is seen clearly, as is.

The self cannot transform itself through effort. The self trying to improve is still the self, thought attempting to manage thought, the observer attempting to change what is observed, becoming attempting to end becoming. The structure remains intact regardless of how sophisticated the approach.

But when conditioning is seen—without judgment, without resistance, without a project attached to the seeing—something shifts naturally.

Take anger. Before seeing, you think: *I shouldn't be angry. Anger is destructive. I need to control this. What's wrong with me?* The self is fighting the anger, which creates a second layer of conflict—anger plus your resistance to anger. Your struggle intensifies, requiring more energy to manage than the original emotion.

With seeing: There is anger. The body is hot. Thought is aggressive. The pattern is visible—not as personal failure, but as a conditioned response to a perceived threat. You experience no resistance. No association. No identification. No urge to fix your anger nor replace it with something more appropriate. Just a clear observation.

And in that seeing—without effort, without management—the anger begins to lose momentum. Not because it was controlled or replaced, but because it was no longer being fed by resistance and identification. The energy your resistance was supplying was withdrawn. The pattern can run its course and pass.

The seeing itself is the recognition.

This is the paradox: the moment you try to transform, you reinforce the self that believes transformation is needed. The moment you stop trying and simply see what is actually present—without the agenda of fixing it—transformation occurs on its own, in its own time, as a natural consequence of clarity rather than as an achievement of effort.

ELEVATED AWARENESS IS A CLEARING, NOT A CLIMB

Elevated awareness is not a state you achieve by ascending. It is what remains when conditioning is no longer occupying all available attention.

Awareness requires space. When conditioning dominates—when thought, interpretation, identification, and the constant self-referencing of the loop consume all available mental space—awareness is crowded out. Not blocked by force. Simply left with no room to operate.

When conditioning is seen clearly, space naturally opens. In this context, elevation doesn't mean rising upward; it means clearing away what was crowding your attention.

Consider a walk through a park. Before seeing, your attention is entirely occupied, but not by the nature surrounding you: *I should have said that differently in the meeting. What will they think of me? I need to send that email. Why do I always mess things up this way?* The walk happens. The park is there. But you barely notice it. Thought has occupied every available unit of your attention.

After seeing, thought may still arise—*I should have said that differently*—but it is recognized as thought. Attention is not captured by it in the same way. And in that space, you actually see the park. You have room to notice the light through the leaves, the texture of the path under your feet, the smell of fresh-cut grass, the sound of birds and a dog barking.

Nothing mystical is occurring. Your mind is not elevated in the spiritual-achievement sense. You are simply able to perceive more of what is actually surrounding you—because your attention is no longer entirely occupied by what was.

ONGOING RECOGNITION

What does daily life look like when lived from seeing—not as a continuous state, but as a recurring quality of presence that appears more frequently as conditioning is seen more clearly?

You wake up. A thought arises—perhaps anxiety about the big presentation ahead. You see it as thought. The body sensation is felt—tightness in the chest, shallow breath. You are not consumed by it. You noticed the anxiety. You are aware that the pattern is running. You get up. The day begins.

At work, a colleague dismisses your idea in a meeting. Irritation arises immediately—thought fires: *They never listen. They don't respect me.* But you see the irritation as conditioning responding to perceived threat. The pattern is visible. You can respond without being driven by the urgency to defend or prove. Perhaps you can clarify your point. Perhaps you let it pass. But your response comes from clarity, not from the protection of an image that needed defending.

You make a mistake, and a thought fires instantly: *I suck at this.* But you recognize the old groove activating—the familiar pattern that has run for years. You are able to address, correct, and learn from the mistake without collapsing into feelings of inadequacy. You are aware you made a mistake, and it does not confirm a fundamental truth about who you are.

You receive good news. Excitement arises. But you are not inflated by it. Success does not define you any more than failure does. The news is registered. Life continues.

You face uncertainty. The known offers no clear answer. The situation is genuinely unclear. Instead of panic, instead of thought desperately grasping for certainty that isn't available, there is space. Not knowing becomes tolerable. You observe. You act when clarity arises, not before. And you do not need absolute certainty to function.

This is living from seeing. Not perfection. Not enlightenment. Not the end of conditioning or the permanent disappearance of the loop. It is clarity appearing where identification once ruled—again and again, in ordinary moments, as ordinary life unfolds.

THE LAKE

A stone is thrown. Ripples spread. The reflection fragments.

You don't force stillness. You watch—because you recognize the difference between the movement on the surface and the depth that contains it.

Thought arises. Emotion moves. Conditioning activates. Old patterns fire. These are movements within experience. They are not definitions of it. They are not what nor who you are.

Ripples pass—not because they are resisted, but because movement completes itself when it isn't fed. Clarity returns, not as an achievement nor as a reward, but merely as what remains when your interference ends.

When the stone is thrown again, ripples will return. Seeing may or may not be present in the next moment. This is not a failure, but the ordinary movement of a conditioned mind operating in a complex world.

But once the difference between the surface and the depth has been recognized—even once, even briefly—the relationship to disturbance is never quite the same.

Because you know something that cannot be unknown: the disturbance and the depth that contains it are not the same thing. And you are no longer the disturbance.

Is there anything present right now—some thought, some tension, some subtle urgency—that you have been carrying without noticing? Pay attention to that feeling. Not because something needs to be done about it. Just to see it. To recognize: this is happening. This is movement within awareness. This feeling is not what I am. Just allow yourself that simple seeing. Nothing more is needed.

Beyond Intellectual Understanding

You stand at the edge of a cliff.

Behind you lies familiar territory—mapped, named, predictable. The known: every belief accumulated, every interpretation stored, every identity formed and defended. The known provides continuity, familiarity, and the sense of a self that persists across time.

Ahead is only space.

Thought wants to build a bridge across the gap. The self wants to retreat to what it already knows. Conditioning seeks to translate the unfamiliar into something it can recognize and categorize. But none of that is happening yet. You are simply here—at the edge, where certainty ends.

Part Two has clarified something that cannot be unseen now that you're aware of it.

Intellectual understanding is not the same as seeing. They are not different degrees of the same thing—they are different in kind.

Intellectual understanding accumulates in memory. That understanding is available under calm conditions—present when the system is settled, absent when it is most needed. Intellectual understanding can describe suffering with precision and yet find no way to ease it. Your intellect can explain the loop in detail while remaining entirely inside it. Intellectual understanding is produced by the known, and the known cannot step outside itself to see itself.

Seeing operates differently. Seeing does not add to the known. Seeing alters your relationship to what is already there. When conditioning is seen directly—without judgment, without resistance, without a project attached to the seeing—something shifts that understanding alone cannot produce. The seeing itself is the recognition. Not a preparation for it. Not a step toward it. The recognition occurs as a natural consequence of clarity.

> *Becoming cannot end becoming. Effort cannot end effort. The self cannot transcend itself through the self's own methods. But seeing—direct, undefended, without agenda—changes your relationship to the whole loop. And changing the relationship is all that is needed.*

When thought is recognized as thought, its authority over behavior loosens. When the observer is recognized as the observed, the division that creates the watcher and the watched collapses. When effort is seen as unnecessary—not abandoned out of laziness, but released through understanding so complete that effort is revealed as the obstacle rather than the solution—awareness, which was always present, becomes accessible again.

You now understand the mechanism completely. You can recognize conditioning as it arises. You know the difference between conceptual knowledge and direct perception. You have seen the subtle trap of striving toward spiritual identity—the way the self repurposes even insight as material for a new version of becoming.

But understanding alone is not liberation. Understanding is the ground from which something else becomes possible.

The question that naturally arises here—the one that has been implicit throughout this entire section is: *if the self cannot produce seeing through effort or method or becoming, how does seeing actually occur?*

The answer is paradoxical, and it must be stated plainly.

There is no movement toward seeing. Movement belongs to becoming. Becoming belongs to psychological time. Seeing occurs when that movement ends—not through a decision to stop, but through the recognition that the movement has an agenda: **to perpetuate itself.**

When the effort to be aware relaxes, awareness is present. When the known is no longer being defended, extended, and projected into the future, what lies beyond the known is not revealed as something new, but is simply no longer obscured. This is not passivity nor indifference to life nor withdrawal from engagement. This ability to see, this clarity, is the end of internal conflict—and internal conflict, as Part One established, is not the same as engagement with life. Internal conflict, as one of the root causes of human struggle, is the cost of being fully alive.

The self cannot cross the threshold that leads beyond itself. The self is made of the known. At the point where becoming stops, or even pauses, the self has nowhere to go. What remains is what has been present throughout—the awareness that emerges when the self is absent. That awareness is not the product of the self; it is what's possible when your attention stops being occupied by the movement of your thoughts.

Part Three explores what remains when the known no longer dominates perception—when identity loosens further, when the belief in a fixed psychological center weakens, when seeing is no longer resisted because there is no longer a self urgently trying to improve itself.

This is not just another philosophy. It is a lived inquiry.

The terrain you have been walking ends here. Everything behind you belongs to the known—memory, explanation, structure. Beyond this edge is something you cannot enter through intellectual understanding alone.

What becomes clear here is simple: the edge was never a boundary to cross. It was the point at which illusion becomes visible. And once visible, it can no longer hold the same authority it held when it was simply mistaken for reality.

Living Without Separation

CHAPTER 10

The Unknown

An innocent child sees snow for the first time.

She has no word for it,
no memory to compare it to,
no story about what "snow" means.

She just sees white flakes falling,
feels cold touching her skin,
experiences wonder without explanation.

This is pure contact with what is
—before thought names it,
before memory claims it.

This is the unknown.

Part Two ended at the edge of a cliff—the edge of what understanding can carry you to. You have seen the mechanism. You have recognized the gap between knowing and seeing. You have watched conditioning operate more clearly than before. But seeing opens onto something. This chapter moves into that territory—not to take you to a new destination, but to show you what is already here when the filter of the known loosens its insistence on being everything.

BEYOND THE KNOWN

What you encountered from seeing was not distance from life, but greater intimacy with it—experience met more directly, without the constant mediation of interpretation and identity standing between you and what is actually happening.

But there is a territory beyond even that—beyond the quieting of reactivity, beyond the loosening of identification, beyond the moment-to-moment recognition of the loop. This is the territory the entire book has been moving toward without yet naming it directly.

The unknown is not beyond reach, and it is not mysterious or reserved for those who have practiced long enough. It is, in a precise sense, the most ordinary thing possible.

The child, seeing snow for the first time, does not ask what it is. There is no comparison, no reference point, no expectation shaping the encounter. Cold touches the skin. White falls from the sky. The child experiences movement, sensation, and wonder—without any need for commentary. The experience does not belong to the child. There is no one standing apart from it, deciding what it means or storing it for later evaluation. There is simply direct contact.

Later, language arrives. The word snow is learned. Memory forms. Meaning accumulates—winter, inconvenience, beauty, danger, childhood, nostalgia. Eventually, snow is no longer encountered directly. Every interaction is filtered through what is already known. What was once immediate now becomes mediated. The snow does not change, but the encounter does.

This chapter begins at the point where mediation loosens— where experience is no longer immediately buried inside what has already been learned--where we see what emerges when the obstruction is no longer in the way.

THE MISUNDERSTANDING OF THE UNKNOWN

The very word unknown carries tension.

For most people, the unknown signals uncertainty, instability, or loss of control. Our thoughts treat the unknown as a problem to solve or a territory to avoid. The self responds predictably—by retreating into familiarity or comparison, or by attempting to conquer the unknown through explanation, belief, method, or practice.

In this way, the unknown is almost always misunderstood before it is even encountered.

The unknown is assumed to be mysterious, distant, or elevated—something hidden behind sufficient effort, reserved for those who are disciplined or prepared enough to receive it. Someone hears about living from the unknown and thought constructs an assignment: *I need to meditate more. I need to be in control of my mind. I need to transcend my thoughts.* The unknown becomes a destination, and the self becomes the traveler trying to reach it.

These interpretations feel natural, but they share a common structure: thought is attempting to convert the unknown into something it can manage and approach on its own terms.

But what if the unknown is not something else? What if it is simply life as it is—before memory interprets it, before identity claims it, before meaning solidifies around it?

The unknown feels distant only because the known is so active, so immediate, so total in its occupation of attention. When thought quiets—even briefly—the unknown is not revealed as if uncovered. The unknown was never hidden. The unknown is simply what remains when the filter of accumulated memory is not operating at full intensity. What has always been here was present before the filter arrived to convert it into the known.

EXPERIENCE WITHOUT FILTER

The unknown is experience without the filter of accumulated knowledge.

When you walk into a room you have never been in before, there is a moment—often fleeting—before thought categorizes: *Small. Bright. Reminds me of somewhere. I like it. I don't like it.* In that brief moment before interpretation arrives, there is direct perception. That perception is not enhanced by the interpretation that follows, but replaced by it.

The moment thought intervenes, labeling and comparing and judging, the unknown recedes, and the known takes its place. The room is still there. But what is seen is no longer the room—it is what thought has made of the room.

The same movement occurs inwardly.

When sadness arises and is met without explanation—without resistance, without the story of what it means about you or your life—there is direct contact with what is. That contact is not detached or clinical. That direct contact with what is is intimate, alive, and immediate. Direct perception is unclaimed. There is no one standing outside it, deciding what category it belongs to or what it proves.

The unknown is not elsewhere. It is what remains when experience is not immediately converted into meaning.

This is why the unknown cannot be sought. Seeking belongs entirely to the known, and it is driven by memory, fueled by desire, projected from the past into the future. The unknown is encountered only when the movement of seeking falls quiet. And that quieting cannot be forced. It occurs when the mechanism of seeking is seen clearly—not as something wrong, but as unnecessary.

WHAT LIVES IN QUIET

When thought quiets, not through suppression but genuinely, what becomes available is not emptiness.

Something is present in that quiet that thinking cannot produce and cannot examine, because the act of examination converts it back into the known. That quiet space is not a feeling, not a state, not an experience that can be described and stored for later comparison. It is more fundamental than any of those things.

Some call it intelligence. Some call it the life force itself, before interpretation. Some point toward it by noting that every genuine creative insight, every moment of real clarity, every decision that turned out to be truly right—arrived in the spaces when the mind is still, and when the mind stops insisting on its own conclusions.

This is not mystical. The surgeon who operates with complete stillness of attention, the musician absorbed so completely in the playing that he feels like there is no player, the parent who responds to a child's distress with perfectly calibrated presence—none of these involve the accumulation of more knowledge. They involve the temporary absence of the self's interference.

What becomes available in that absence is what has always been available. It was simply inaccessible while thought was consuming all your mental space.

> *The unknown is not a destination. It is not something to seek or practice toward. It is what is already here when the movement of seeking stops. In this very moment—before any conclusion is drawn about what this means—the unknown is present.*

WHY THE SELF HAS NO ROLE HERE

The self is composed entirely of the known.

The self exists as memory, identity, and psychological time, which is always looking to the past or projecting into the future. Its function is to orient, to predict, to protect continuity. These functions are practical and necessary within their domain—but they reach a natural boundary. At the point where orientation fails, where there is nothing to reference, no position to maintain, no outcome to secure—the self has no role to play.

Consider a moment of complete, genuine uncertainty. You face a situation with no clear answer. The known offers nothing—no past experience that fits, no identity to guide you, no formula to apply. The self tries to function: *What should I do? What would someone like me choose? What is the safest option?* But none of these questions resolves anything. They only produce more thought.

Eventually, if the self's movement is seen clearly, there is a pause. One does not make a decision to pause—one merely recognizes that the self cannot solve this, combined with the understanding that the self's inability to solve one's uncertainty does not mean it cannot be met. And in that pause—when the self's constant orientation has momentarily stilled—what remains is simply the situation as it is. No overlay. No interpretation. Direct contact with what is actually present.

This is not a problem. It is the natural condition of a mind that has stopped insisting the known must answer everything.

Practical knowledge remains available. Memory continues to function when required. But it no longer dominates perception. Life is met directly—without the constant overlay of interpretation that converts every experience into evidence for a conclusion already formed.

WHOLENESS IS NOT ACHIEVED— IT IS RECOGNIZED

Here is the most direct statement this book can make about where all of this has been leading.

Wholeness is not something to arrive at. Wholeness is not the reward at the end of sufficient practice or the result of finally understanding the mechanism clearly enough. Wholeness is not a state to be cultivated and maintained.

Wholeness is what emerges when the confusion that obscures it is no longer operating.

The sense of incompleteness—the persistent feeling of not yet being whole, not yet having arrived, not yet being enough— is not a fact about your actual condition. That sense of incompleteness is a structural consequence of living from the known. The self is fragmented by design because incompleteness is what generates the movement of becoming that sustains it. A self that arrived would have no function. So the self perpetually defers arrival.

But beneath the self's perpetual motion, beneath the becoming and the seeking and the improving—something else has always been present. Something that was never in the process of becoming anything. Something that was never incomplete.

This is what the child touched in her first experience with snow—not because the child was advanced or enlightened, but simply because the machinery that generates incompleteness had not yet fully formed in her. She was able to meet the snow directly. Nothing was lacking. The moment was complete as it was.

That same completeness is available to you now. Not as a memory of a purer time, not as a state to recover, but as the actual ground of this moment—when the movement of becoming is seen for what it is, and the urgency to be something other than what one presently is quietly ceases.

Becoming ends when wholeness is recognized—not when it is achieved. And wholeness cannot be recognized while the self is actively engaged in the project of becoming. The two movements are mutually exclusive. **Wholeness is what remains when becoming stops.**

THE FIRST SNOW RETURNS

The same child stands in the snow again, years later.

Thought arrives immediately: *Snow. Winter. Cold. I need gloves. The roads will be slippery.* The known has done its work. The word came. Memory formed. Meaning accumulated. Function is intact.

But something else is now possible.

The known can be present without consuming everything. Thought names what it sees as snow, but the naming doesn't obscure the white falling. Memory recalls other winters, but the recalling doesn't replace this moment. The accumulation of knowledge about snow does not prevent today's direct encounter with snow.

The unknown was never lost. It was only covered. And when the known loosens its insistence on being all there is— even briefly—what remains is the same direct contact the child once knew: white flakes falling, cold touching skin, wonder without explanation.

Not recovered. Not achieved.

Simply there.

As it always was.

CHAPTER 11

Living in the Space Between

You are standing in a doorway.

Behind you is a familiar room.
Every object has a place.
Every surface has been seen before.
You know where to step without looking.

The room carries memory, familiarity, and orientation.

Ahead is open space. No walls to lean against. No clear boundary to define where you stand. Nothing arranged. Nothing named.

You are not fully in the room.
You are not yet outside it.

You are standing on the threshold.
One foot remains in what is known.
The other rests where certainty no longer applies.

This is not a transition you complete.

It is not a stage you pass through.

This is where you find yourself now.

THE NATURE OF THE SPACE BETWEEN

Living from the unknown does not mean abandoning the known.

Memory does not disappear. Thought does not stop. Skills do not dissolve. Life continues to require language, planning, learning, and decision-making. The known remains entirely available—functional, intelligent, useful for all the purposes for which it was built.

What changes is not what exists. What changes is what governs.

The space between is not a place you enter and remain in permanently. The space between is not a psychological position or a new identity to maintain. The space between is the condition in which the known is available without being absolute, and the unknown is present without being named or sought. Thought arises and is seen as thought. Emotion moves and is felt without becoming identity. Conditioning activates and is recognized without immediately taking control.

Nothing is excluded. Nothing is pursued.

This is the space between—not as a state, but as a living relationship to experience.

THE FELT QUALITY OF LIVING HERE

This space has a distinct texture—though it is nothing like what the seeking self imagined it would feel like.

There is often a sense of openness—not dramatic or expansive, not a peak experience to be chased, but unforced spaciousness. Mental noise does not vanish, yet it no longer fills the entire field of attention. Inner commentary softens. The urgency to define, evaluate, or position oneself loosens without being deliberately relaxed.

Thought still appears, but it is noticed rather than inhabited. Emotion still moves, but it does not immediately construct a story that must be resolved. Anger arises and passes. Sadness moves through. Joy appears without the compulsion to hang onto it before it goes.

Nothing is pushed away. Nothing is held.

You are in a conversation. Someone challenges what you have said. A familiar thought arises: *They are being unfair. Why do they always do this?* You pause—not deliberately, simply because you are present. The thought is recognized as thought. The defensive impulse may still activate, but it does not immediately consume all your attention. Response—or the choice not to respond—comes from clarity rather than from an urgent desire to protect your image.

Life feels less managed. Not because control has been achieved, but because the compulsion to achieve control has weakened. And with that weakening, an unexpected ease appears—not the ease of nothing being difficult, but the ease of finding you are not at war with what is difficult.

NO PSYCHOLOGICAL GROUND

Living in the space between does not involve maintaining awareness or holding a particular posture of mind as a practice. Living here involves noticing when the old reflexes and patterns attempt to reclaim authority—and observing that noticing without judgment.

When you find yourself feeling defensive, you are able to see your defensiveness for what it is. You feel your anxiety as sensation and thought—both real, neither conclusive. You notice a familiar self-image dominating your attention for an afternoon. You recognize the structure, but you feel no requirement to intervene. You also feel no sense of failure if your recognition comes late.

Your judgment of yourself would only create further division. If you made an effort to change your thoughts or feelings, you would only reassert the self's authority. What actually changes here is not the content of experience, but the absence of psychological ownership of that content.

Sadness can be present without becoming the sadness that defines who you are and what your life means. Anger can arise without becoming who you are in this moment. Fear can move through you without requiring an explanation, a solution, or a story about why you shouldn't be feeling this.

This is not detachment. Seeing your script as it runs is intimacy without possession—full contact with your experience without that experience being converted into evidence for your identity.

When you need to take action, the difference in your approach becomes tangible. Action driven by conditioning carries urgency, tension, and self-protection beneath it. You receive a message that requires a response. If conditioning is running, you think: *I need to reply perfectly. What will they think? I cannot look incompetent.* That response is written from self-protection—and is careful, managed, and slightly false.

Without that overlay: you read a message that requires a response, and what you need to communicate becomes clear. You write your response more directly, in a fully proportionate manner, and you do that not because you made more of an effort, but because less interference was present.

The known remains fully functional, but it no longer defines everything.

WHEN CONDITIONING RETURNS

Conditioning does not disappear. This needs to be said plainly, because the expectation that it should disappear is itself a form of becoming—a subtle demand that life conform to what your new insight has promised.

Old pathways reassert themselves under stress. Fatigue narrows attention and makes identification more likely. Strong emotion intensifies the self's grip. None of this indicates regression or failure. Those old pathways reflect the depth at which conditioning was formed—over years, decades, a lifetime of repetition.

What changes is not the absence of reaction, but the timing of recognition.

Where reaction once dominated for days, causing you to seethe, stew, and worry, reaction can now be seen in hours. You receive sharp criticism. The familiar tightening arises—*They are wrong. They don't understand.* Your defensive story begins to assemble. Later that afternoon, you notice: *I have been replaying that conversation for hours.* The pattern is visible to you now, even though it ran for most of the day before recognition arrived.

A month passes. The same pattern activates. This time, your recognition arrives mid-conversation—*there is defensiveness here, happening right now.* Your reaction is already underway, but you can see it as it unfolds rather than after it has fully completed.

Later still, the pattern may be recognized before it takes full hold. You feel the impulse to defend at the moment it arises, before it has gathered the momentum of full identification.

Recognition does not prevent reaction through effort or willpower. Conscious recognition interrupts unconscious reaction. And unconscious reaction, once interrupted regularly, gradually loses the totality of its authority.

Conditioning depends on remaining unseen. Once exposed and seen clearly, without self-judgment, without making the exposure itself into another project, your conditioning cannot operate with the same strength. Once conditioning is no longer invisible, its hold on you weakens.

FUNCTIONING WITHOUT ANCHORING

From the outside, a life lived in this space looks unremarkable.

You wake up. Unconscious thought appears about the day—perhaps a list of tasks, perhaps a trace of anxiety about a meeting. You notice those thoughts without interpretation, without the secondary layer of what this means about how the day will go. The thoughts move, but you are not attracted to them.

At work, someone reacts sharply to something you have said. Defensiveness arises immediately—the body tightens, thought prepares to explain and justify. You feel yourself tense.

You may respond clearly, addressing what was actually said. Or you may react defensively and see it later, recognizing the pattern after it has already run. Neither is evaluated as success or failure. Both are simply what happened.

Choices appear throughout the day. Habit offers familiar paths. Attention remains open to what the situation actually requires rather than defaulting automatically to what you have always done.

In the evening, you may notice where clarity was present and where conditioning took over. You may warmly recall a conversation that flowed without self-consciousness. A decision that was made simply, without inner war. A moment of anxiety that tightened around something uncertain. None of this is evaluated as spiritual progress or evidence of how far you have come. Each moment is seen as it unfolds.

Nothing is concluded. Nothing is resolved into a verdict about where you are.

This is not progress. It is presence without the need for every experience to confirm or construct an identity. Ordinary life continues, moment by moment, without the requirement that life must always mean something about you.

At the end of a day—any day—try noticing without judgment: *Where was the clarity? Where did conditioning run without you noticing?* Notice without evaluating either situation. Don't measure your progress; simply see what was present and what was not, without making a verdict of it. This is the practice that is not a practice—seeing without letting the self score its own performance.

THE DOORWAY REMAINS

You are still in the doorway.

Behind you lies the known—memory, skill, language, identity, everything accumulated, functional, and available when needed. Ahead is the unknown—life meeting itself without psychological mediation, without the self converting each moment into evidence for its own continuity.

There is no requirement to choose between them. Confusion arises only when the belief forms that you must stand entirely in one or the other—that liberation means leaving the known behind forever, or that returning to the known means you failed or that something has been lost.

The doorway is not a compromise. The doorway is not a middle ground between two positions. The doorway is the absence of the need for ground altogether.

Here, the known is visible but no longer absolute. Here, the unknown is present but no longer threatening. Nothing needs to be secured. No threshold needs to be crossed.

You are not moving toward anything. You are simply no longer standing where you once believed you had to.

And in that absence of position, life continues—unclaimed, immediate, and quietly sufficient.

The doorway remains.

The known functions when it is needed.

The unknown is present whenever the known loosens its claim to be everything.

CHAPTER 12

The Center That Was Never There

A spinning top appears stable only while it turns.

As long as motion continues, a center seems to exist—something fixed around which everything else revolves.

But when the spinning slows, the illusion disappears.

There was never a center holding the motion together.

There was only movement.

The sense of a center was created by speed.

Living in the space between—as Chapter 11 described—still carries one unexamined assumption: That there is someone living there. This chapter looks directly at that assumption.

THE SUBTLE OBSERVER

Even now—after all that has been examined—something subtle may remain unquestioned. You may clearly see your thoughts arise and pass. You may recognize emotions as movement rather than identity. You may notice conditioning activate without being immediately captured by it. All of this brings real change— a genuine loosening of the grip that once felt absolute.

But beneath all of it, one assumption often persists untouched:

That there is someone who is seeing.

This assumption is not a declared belief nor something you would insist on if asked. But you believe it as a quiet, background orientation—an unspoken sense that there is an observer standing behind experience, watching thoughts, noticing emotions, being aware of conditioning as it arises.

This chapter does not offer a new insight to accumulate. Instead, it turns attention toward that assumption itself.

Is there actually a seer?

Or has seeing been happening without one all along?

SEEING WITHOUT A CENTER

When a thought arises, it appears spontaneously. It does not announce itself beforehand, nor does it require permission or authorization. When an emotion moves through the body, it is felt directly—not delivered to someone standing apart from it, waiting to receive it. When awareness is present, it does not arrive on cue. It is already here.

So where is the one who sees these things?

What often becomes clear in this looking is that the sense of being a seer is itself a thought—a subtle mental movement that appears after awareness is already present, claiming ownership of what it did not produce. Language reinforces this illusion constantly: I am aware. I am noticing. I am observing. But these phrases are interpretations layered onto experience after the fact. They are not descriptions of what is actually happening in the moment awareness occurs.

Awareness does not need an owner. Seeing does not require a seer.

The idea of a central observer is not discovered through perception. The idea is assumed through thought and then reinforced by the language that thought uses to describe itself.

But when that assumption is examined closely, the observer cannot be found.

AWARENESS WITHOUT OWNERSHIP

When the belief in a separate seer loosens, nothing dramatic occurs. There is no explosion of insight, no altered state to maintain, no experience to chase and replicate.

Life continues.

Thoughts still arise. Emotions still move. Decisions are made. Relationships unfold. Challenges appear. The forms of experience remain unchanged. What changes is the absence of a psychological center organizing it all, referencing everything back to itself, requiring every moment to say something about who is here experiencing it.

You are walking. Your body moves. Thoughts appear—perhaps about the day, perhaps arising without any clear occasion. There is no *I am walking* being continuously affirmed in the background. There is simply: walking happening, thoughts appearing, and awareness present. When thought does construct: *I am walking*, it is seen as another movement—not as confirmation of a central self that must be maintained.

Experience is no longer referenced back to an internal me who must interpret, defend, or manage what is happening. Thoughts are no longer my thoughts in the old possessive sense that made them urgent. Emotions are no longer my emotions requiring a verdict. Action no longer requires a doer standing behind it, monitoring whether it is being done correctly and what it reveals about the doer.

There is no replacement for the self. Nothing steps in to take its place. There is simply experience, happening. Awareness, present. Life, unfolding.

This is not emptiness. This dissolution is not detachment or withdrawal. This dissolution is not coldness or indifference. What remains is life without the added layer of psychological ownership—full, immediate, alive, but unclaimed.

And with the collapse of that center, psychological suffering loses its foundation. Pain still occurs. Loss still hurts. Difficulty still arises and demands a response. But the inner resistance, the self-talk that says, *"this shouldn't be happening, not to me, not again"*— falls away. Not because it was suppressed. Because there is no longer a me at the center wishing the world would be other than it is.

> *Try this, not as a meditation exercise but as a genuine inquiry: Notice a sound. Whatever sound is present right now—traffic, a hum, the quality of silence itself. The sound is heard. Awareness is present. But who is listening? If you look for the one who is hearing—not conceptually, but as direct investigation—what do you find?*

Thought may immediately construct: *I am hearing this.* But that thought came after the hearing. The hearing was already complete before I claimed it.

If you look directly, can you locate an observer that is separate from what is being observed? Is there a boundary where awareness ends and a me begins? Is there an internal entity behind experience, or only experience itself unfolding, with awareness present throughout?

EXPERIENCE WITHOUT A "ME"

I must take care to be precise here, because this territory is easily misunderstood in ways that create new forms of the old problem.

When the self falls away, nothing replaces it.

There is no higher identity, no truer version of you, no expanded sense of "I" that takes the place of the striving self. Awareness does not become a new self. Consciousness does not become a new center around which experience is now organized at a more elevated level. Any such replacement would simply rebuild the structure that you have seen through, just with more spiritually respectable content.

What dissolves is not functioning, personality, or the particular human being you are. What dissolves is the belief that there was ever an independent entity at the center of your experience — separate from what it was experiencing, requiring that experience to confirm its existence and meaning.

You still have preferences. You still make choices. Someone asks: *want to go get ice cream?* Your response comes naturally—*yes, or no, thanks.* There is no inner consultation, no *I should, or I shouldn't* deliberating with itself. The preference is simply present. Function continues without requiring a central self to authorize it.

The self was never an essence. The self was a pattern—repetitive thought mistaken for a permanent identity. When that mistake is no longer sustained, nothing needs to be added. Life does not need a new reference point to continue. Experience does not need an owner to unfold.

> *Seeing does not reveal what you are. It reveals that the question—what am I? who am I?—was built on a false assumption. There was never a fixed thing to be found. There was only awareness, and the thought that something was standing behind it.*

NO ONE LEFT TO CONTINUE SEEKING

There is no conclusion to draw, no state to stabilize, no insight to carry forward as a new identity.

The movement of becoming has simply lost its urgency—because the one who was doing the becoming has been seen to be a process rather than a fact.

Life continues—open, immediate, flowing. The known still functions where it is useful. Memory, language, and skill remain available. The unknown remains present as direct contact with what is, moment by moment, before thought converts it into something already known.

Nothing needs to be reconciled between the known and the unknown.

Preferences exist without an owner. Choices are made without a decision maker standing outside them. Action happens without a doer at the center directing each movement and monitoring whether it reflects well on them. This is not passivity—it is function without the constant overlay of me managing, evaluating, and protecting every movement.

The search ends—not because something was found at the destination where the search was aimed, but because the one who was searching is no longer assumed to be the entity the self was searching for.

And when that assumption falls away, what remains is simply this: life, happening. Awareness, present. Nothing missing.

THE HORIZON

The horizon appears to separate the earth and the sky. From a distance, it looks like a boundary—a line you could reach if you walked far enough. But the closer you move toward it, the more it recedes. The line was never a place. It was a perspective.

The sense of a self is like that horizon. Your self seemed to mark a center of experience, a point from which life was viewed and organized. But when approached directly—when looked for rather than assumed—that center could never be found. Because the self was never there in the way it appeared to be.

There is no edge to cross. No threshold requiring a final act of surrender. No moment at which the self is officially dissolved and something new begins.

Instead, you have only the quiet recognition that life has always been happening without a fixed center. That awareness has always been present without anyone owning it. The moment you are in has always been complete.

And once you recognize this, the ending is also the beginning.

There is simply what has always been—clear, immediate, and uncontained.

> *Right now—not as an exercise, but as genuinely looking—can you find the edge of awareness? Where does it begin? Where does it end? Is there a place where awareness stops and something outside it starts? Or is awareness simply here, without a boundary, without anyone at the center claiming it? Not as a state to achieve. As the simplest fact of this moment.*

CHAPTER 13

Relationship Without Separation

A shadow stretches across the ground.

*It appears solid, definite, with clear edges that
separate it from the light around it.*
*It moves when objects move, changes shape when
angles shift and seems to have its own distinct
existence.*

*From this perspective, you could imagine the
shadow believes it is independent. It defines itself
against the brightness. It clings to the light that
gives it definition, and yet believes itself to be
independent from it.*

Then, without drama, something is seen.

*The shadow recognizes it has never existed apart
from light.*

*Nothing extraordinary happens. The shadow does
not vanish. It still darkens the ground. It still
shifts and changes. But the belief in opposition
ends,
and with it, the struggle that belief produced.*

This is not transcendence. It is recognition.
*And recognition changes the relationship—not by
adding something new, but by removing what
was never real.*

When the center dissolves—as Chapter 12 examined—what changes is not only internal. The dissolution of psychological separation reshapes every relationship it touches. This chapter examines how.

BEYOND INDIVIDUAL FREEDOM

Human life does not unfold in isolation. The self was never only an internal structure—it expressed itself outward, through every relationship, every conversation, every moment of connection and conflict and withdrawal.

When identification with thought loosens, when the psychological center dissolves, when seeing operates more consistently, something shifts not just inwardly but in every relationship that surrounds it. The change moves outward, not because it was aimed outward, but because the structure that produced separation is no longer operating in the same way.

So, the question naturally arises: what happens in relationships when the illusion of separation is seen through?

This is not a moral question. The answer is not about becoming kinder, more patient, or more loving through effort and intention. This is a structural question. When the psychological center that organized experience dissolves, the relationship reorganizes itself—not by intention, not by effort, but because the mechanism that created the division is no longer the totality.

HOW SEPARATION OPERATES IN RELATIONSHIP

The self is not just a personal identity. The self is also a structure of division.

The self exists through contrast—me and you, right and wrong, inside and outside, safe and threatening. The self stabilizes itself through comparison, judgment, and defense. When this structure enters a relationship, it turns connection into negotiation.

At a subtle level, even love becomes conditional without anyone intending it. The self seeks confirmation through the other: *See me the way I need to be seen. Do not threaten my image. Validate my worth. Do not abandon me. Do not reject me.* These are not conscious demands. They are the self's conditioning seeking continuity through another person.

This is why relationships become transactional even when deep affection is present. This is why communication becomes distorted even between people who genuinely care about each other. This is why disagreement so reliably feels personal. This is why intimacy carries fear beneath the closeness—because to be truly known is to risk the self revealing itself as it is.

The self does not truly relate, and it protects itself through relationships. As long as this structure dominates, the relationship cannot be whole. The relationship can be meaningful, loyal, and sincere—and still remain fundamentally organized around psychological separation. Two people trying to meet through their conditioning, each one reaching for the other through the lens of what they need the other to be.

LOVE AS A BY-PRODUCT OF THE UNKNOWN

Here is the most precise thing this book can say about love—and it differs from every other way the word is usually used.

Love, in the sense being recognized here, is not a feeling. Love is not a virtue to be practiced. Love is not an attitude to cultivate nor a commitment to maintain through effort. Cultivated compassion fails when attempted prematurely—the self cannot manufacture what contradicts its own structure. The self can perform kindness, but it cannot produce wholeness. The self can practice patience, but it cannot produce the absence of division that makes a genuine connection.

Love, in this sense, is a by-product of the unknown.

Love appears naturally when the psychological separation that prevents it is seen through. Not as something added to experience, not as something achieved after sufficient practice, but as what was always present beneath the structure of division—the way warmth is what remains when cold is removed.

When the self is seen clearly—when judgment loses its foundation because you have watched the same mechanism operate in yourself that you are judging in another—something shifts in the quality of perception. Their defensiveness is the same self-protection you have seen in yourself. Their anxiety is the same fear of uncertainty you have felt. Their need to be right is the same attempt to stabilize identity you have watched dissolve in yourself in moments of clarity.

You cannot condemn with the same full force what you have now recognized in yourself.

This is not tolerance. This is not the suppression of judgment. This is the recognition that what you thought you were judging was never what it appeared to be. What you were seeing was conditioning, seeking continuity, and operating as automatically in others as it operated in you.

With this clarity, what prevents love from emerging dissolves. And what remains—when that dissolution is genuine—needs no name and requires no cultivation.

> *Love is not a thing you acquire through cultivation. Love is what remains when the structure that prevented it is seen through. Love cannot be produced by effort nor manufactured by practice. Love is the natural condition of a mind no longer at war with itself—and therefore no longer at war with anything it encounters.*

WHAT HAPPENS IN RELATIONSHIPS WHEN SEPARATION ENDS

The change in relationship does not follow a moral sequence. It follows a structural one and unfolds in stages that are less dramatic than expected and more lasting.

First, space appears where reaction used to be immediate. You notice defensiveness arising rather than becoming it. You notice the impulse to correct, withdraw, dominate, or perform—and the noticing creates a gap where the impulse used to fire immediately into action. The self still appears, but it no longer operates invisibly.

Then, responsibility becomes obvious without guilt. Blame loses its grip—not because you decide to stop blaming, but because the mechanism is too clearly seen to sustain the illusion that others are causing your reactions. Conditioning is recognized as conditioning. You stop demanding that the world arrange itself differently so that you can remain undisturbed.

As your acceptance and clear seeing stabilizes, perception genuinely widens. You begin to hear what someone is actually saying rather than only processing other's words through how they affect your image. You can remain present inside disagreement without it collapsing into right and wrong. Complexity becomes tolerable because identity is no longer at stake in the outcome.

Finally, the sense of threat in difference dissolves. Differences remain—preferences, boundaries, values, everything that makes two people distinct. But the psychological weight of those differences lightens. You see that most human behavior is conditioning seeking to protect itself. And once you have seen this clearly in yourself, you will start to recognize it in others—which makes all kinds of previously intolerable behavior easier to accept.

This does not make you passive or without preferences. This makes you present—able to engage with what is actually here, rather than with the story the self was generating about what it means.

ACTION WITHOUT FRAGMENTATION

When the psychological center loosens, the character of action changes.

Before seeing, action carried the weight of the self in every movement. Every decision was filtered through: *What does this say about me? What will they think of me? Am I doing this correctly?* Even generous action had a hidden layer—to confirm worth, to be seen as someone who helps, to protect the self-image of a good person.

After seeing, action simplifies. Action does not become effortless in the physical sense—work still requires effort; difficulty still requires engagement. But the psychological overlay lightens.

You help because the situation calls for it—not to confirm that you are a helpful person. You speak because something needs to be said—not to manage how you are perceived. You act and then release—without monitoring the outcome to confirm that you did it right and that the right person noticed.

This is not detachment. You fully engage with the action— you are more fully engaged than before, because no part of your attention is split between what is happening and what it means about you. There is only the action itself, meeting the situation to which it is responding.

Action without fragmentation is met directly without distortion. The situation presents itself. Clarity meets it. The right responses emerge.

WHOLENESS IN RELATIONSHIP

Here is the most practical truth of this chapter: *You cannot give what you do not embody.*

When the self is fragmented—caught in its own becoming, defending its image, seeking confirmation through others— whatever is offered carries that fragmentation within it. Need disguised as affection. Judgment disguised as concern. Control disguised as care. The other person feels it, even when they cannot name it. The contact is there, but something beneath the contact is managed.

When internal conflict diminishes—when the self is no longer at war with its own experience—something else becomes possible.

A friend calls, distressed. Before seeing: part of your attention is elsewhere, monitoring how you appear as a listener, preparing advice that confirms your value, feeling faintly burdened by the weight of someone else's difficulty. The conversation happens, but your energy is split between the friend and your own image of yourself as someone who helps.

After seeing, the call is simply received. The distress is heard without an agenda. No part of your attention is managing the interaction for what it reflects back. The friend feels met—not because you tried harder or deployed better listening techniques, but because you were actually there. Your attention was undivided.

From that presence, the relationship reorganizes itself. You do not decide to be compassionate—compassion appears. You do not try to listen—listening happens. You do not aim to connect—connection occurs, because the structure that prevented it is no longer operating with full authority.

This is how transformation becomes relational. Not through persuasion or teaching or consciously modeling a better way of being. Through presence. A mind no longer at war with itself creates less war in everything it touches—quietly, structurally, inevitably.

WHAT THE SHADOW KNOWS

The shadow still moves across the ground. The shadow still changes with every shift in angle, every movement of form.

But something fundamental has changed.

The shadow no longer believes it exists in contrast to light. The shadow no longer defines itself against brightness. The shadow no longer experiences itself as separate from the light that was always its source.

The shadow has recognized what it has always been: light contrasting with form. Not light's opposite. Light's expression.

You do not stop having preferences in relationships. You do not stop having boundaries or responding to what harms or nourishes. Life continues with all its complexity, all its texture, all its movement, difficulty, and beauty.

But the psychological war ends.

You stop defending an image that was never real. You stop demanding that others confirm what you cannot confirm in yourself. You stop treating connection as negotiation and intimacy as a contract with hidden clauses.

You do not become extraordinary. You do not withdraw from relationships into some protected interior state. You do not escape life.

You simply stop believing you are separate from it.

And when that belief ends—when the shadow recognizes its source—what remains is not emptiness.

> *Wholeness is not a state to maintain. It is the natural condition of life when it is no longer filtered through division. Wholeness was not somewhere ahead of you. It was never absent. It was simply obscured— by the structure of the self, by the movement of becoming, by the belief that something was still missing. When that belief ceases, the wholeness that has always been there becomes visible.*

This is not the end of relationships. This is the beginning of meeting relationships without distortion.

The shadow knows its source now.

And in that knowing, the struggle to be separate—from light, from life, from what has always been—dissolves.

Not through effort. Not through time.

Through recognition.

And recognition is instant.

The Art of Living

The movement of this book may have felt, at times, like a descent into darkness—the mechanism of the self laid bare, suffering shown to be structural, every familiar attempt at improvement revealed as another expression of what the self was striving to resolve.

But what appeared as darkness was never a substance in itself. Darkness was not something added to the experience. Darkness was the absence of clear seeing. Not the presence of something wrong—the absence of something that was always already available when the mind was clear and still.

Nothing needed to be illuminated. Nothing needed to be brought in from outside. What changed was not the presence of light. What changed was the removal of what was obscuring it.

This synthesis does not mark completion or attainment. This synthesis marks the end of a specific misunderstanding.

What has been clarified is not what you must become. What has been clarified is what you are not.

You are not the thought that arises automatically from memory. You are not the body's faithful execution of signals it received from an old management system. You are not the self that assembled itself through repetition and has been defending its image ever since. You are not even the observer standing behind experience, watching it all unfold.

These are processes. They arise. They pass. They were never you, but the confusion between them and what you actually are was the source of all the suffering this book examined.

> *Wholeness was never something to become. Wholeness was what was present before becoming began—and what is present now, when the movement of becoming is seen clearly enough to pause it.*

Viewed as a whole, the book resolves into a single coherent movement.

Part One revealed the mechanism: suffering is structurally created—not personal failure, not weakness, but an automatic system operating beneath awareness, generating the continuous experience of incompleteness.

Part Two revealed why understanding alone cannot produce the shift it describes—intellectual knowledge accumulates in memory and remains available only when the system is calm, while seeing operates beneath the self's methods entirely. The self cannot produce seeing through effort, practice, or becoming. But when the movement of seeking is recognized as seeking, something that no amount of understanding could generate becomes possible: a direct perception that changes the relationship to the entire loop.

Part Three moved into what lies beyond that gap: the unknown as direct experience rather than concept, living from the space between as ordinary life rather than achievement, the center of experience examined and found to have no independent substance, and relationship seen as the place where the dissolution of separation becomes most tangible and most alive.

Becoming ends when wholeness is recognized—not when wholeness is achieved. Achievement belongs to psychological time. Recognition happens in this moment, or it does not happen. And in this moment, exactly as it is, nothing is missing.

The sense that something is missing is itself a thought, an idea arising from the self's structure. That thought arises automatically. That thought is not reporting on the actual condition of what is present. That thought is the self doing what it always does: *generating incompleteness to sustain the movement of becoming.*

When that is seen clearly—not intellectually understood but seen—the seeking quiets. Not because the self found something it was seeking, but because the one who was seeking is recognized as never having been incomplete to begin with.

What remains when seeking ends is not a special state. What remains is not elevated, permanent, or mysterious. What remains is life in true simplicity—immediate, alive, complete as it is.

This is what was always here.

This is what the book was always pointing toward.

Not further ahead. Not achievable through more effort or practice.

> *Here. Now. As this moment is—before thought says what is wrong with it, before becoming says what it should be instead, before the self insists on one more step before arrival. This is stillness, and only in that still space is wholeness possible.*

If you read these pages with attention to direct experience—observing your reactions, noticing your patterns, recognizing your moments of awareness—then something has already occurred within you. Not as an event to be recorded and claimed, but as an erosion of false certainty about what you are and what you lack.

Seeing changes the trajectory, not the existence, of psychological patterns. Conditioning does not end. Unconscious identification is simply interrupted more often and more quickly. There is no final immunity. No permanent clarity to be claimed and carried. Seeing is not something achieved once and retained—it is an ongoing recognition that must remain alive, in each moment, as experience actually occurs. Just like breathing.

Nothing here demands adoption. Nothing requires confirmation or agreement.

If recognition has occurred, it does not announce itself. Recognition expresses as simplicity—reduced inner friction, greater tolerance for not knowing, less urgency to convert every moment into evidence of who you are.

If recognition has not yet occurred, nothing has failed. The territory remains. The movement of observation is always available: see what arises, notice identification as it tightens, recognize the loop completing itself. And allow what is seen to be sufficient—without turning the seeing into another project aimed at a future arrival.

What could be explained has been explained.

What remains cannot be carried forward as knowledge. It can only be met, moment by moment, as life unfolds.

Nothing has been gained. Nothing has been achieved.

What was illusory has been recognized.

And that recognition, when alive, is enough.

Conclusion

If anything has shifted in you, that shift did not occur because of your agreement or belief. This shift occurred through observation and constant self-reflection, through seeing what was already operating within you from moment to moment, through noticing what is possible when your attention is not focused on the self's continuous activity.

Your seeing is not owed to any book, author, system, or teaching. At any given moment, insight either occurred—or it did not. If it occurred, it requires no reinforcement. If it did not, nothing has gone wrong. The territory does not close. Conditioning will continue to arise. Thought will resume its familiar patterns. Identification will return—sometimes fully, sometimes briefly, sometimes in forms so subtle that it takes time to recognize them. None of this contradicts what you have seen. These movements are part of the human structure. They were never the problem.

The only illusion that sustains your sense of incompleteness is the belief that these movements were you. That your thoughts were reality. That the pattern was the person. That the self, with its perpetual becoming and its desperate incompleteness, was what you actually are.

When that belief loosens—even briefly, even partially, even in one specific moment with one specific pattern—clarity is present. Not as an experience to hold onto. As the simple absence of confusion. Nothing special. Nothing elevated. Just the ordinary fact of awareness unobstructed.

You were never not whole.

Your wholeness was not hidden behind the conditioning. Wholeness was not located somewhere ahead of the becoming. Wholeness was not waiting at the end of a path that required more knowledge, more practice, more effort.

Wholeness was here. Wholeness is here. Before the first word of this book and after the last word is finished. Wholeness shows up when you are not interfering.

Life will continue as it always has—events unfolding, emotions moving, decisions arising, relationships changing, difficulties appearing and passing and appearing again. What may be different is not life itself, but your relationship to it. And even that difference need not be named, maintained, or defended.

This book does not ask you to follow anybody. This book does not ask you to become someone else. This book does not ask you to continue seeking a journey, measuring your progress, or returning to its pages for confirmation.

This book ends by stepping aside.

What remains is not a teaching. What remains is what has always been here—before the first page was opened and after the last page is closed.

Nothing further needs to be added.

Acknowledgements

To **Kam Bains**—your talent, patience, flexibility, and calm professionalism throughout this process have been extraordinary. You took my vision and gave it a face. Thank you for your beautiful work and for never once making me feel like the challenges we faced were anything other than part of the journey.

To **Lanette Sweeney**—you took my greatest writing disadvantage and turned it into something I could be proud of. Your editorial care and your generous spirit have left their mark on every page of this book.

To **Kevan and Cody**—your very existence inspires me to be a better parent and a better human being. Everything I do, I do with both of you in mind. Both of you are enough and lovable just as you are. Life is a gift, and so are both of you!

To **my mother**, you have my deepest respect. Your courage, thoughtfulness, and unconditional love have been a quiet source of warmth and safety throughout my life—like a secure blanket I could always return to. Your acceptance has taught me what it means to feel seen, supported, and free to become who I need to be.

To **Stephen**, may your heart be filled with love, your soul with passion, and your mind with peace.

To the **friends** who stood by me throughout this journey—you read the early pages, gave me honest feedback, kept telling me this was the right path, and never doubted me or my ability to complete this project. You know who you are. My heart goes out to every one of you.

And to every reader who picked up this book—thank you for your attention. It is the most precious thing you could have given this book and yourself.

About the Author

River Crane is a conscious parent, a licensed Rapid Transformational Therapy practitioner, and an independent consciousness researcher who has spent the past decade exploring the structure of the human psyche—how it forms, how it operates in daily life, and how understanding the self dissolves the need to continually seek self-improvement or to become someone else.

After years of studying the relationship between brain, body, and consciousness—and through direct observation of the mind in daily life—River experienced a fundamental shift that brought her a natural sense of clarity and wholeness.

For the past six years, River has lived from the recognition this book describes—not as theory or borrowed philosophy, but as lived experience. This book grew out of years of self-inquiry and reflection, and from listening to many practitioners who had glimpsed wholeness but struggled to sustain it. Again and again, River saw that what was missing was not another technique, but a clear understanding of the structure of the self.

River lives in Utah with her family, where these insights continue to inform her daily life, relationships, and work with clients.